MW01515390

Overcoming The Nine-to-Five System

"The Afflatus Moment"

OVERCOMING THE NINE-TO-FIVE SYSTEM

"The Afflatus Moment"

MICHAEL ARNOLD

Mill City Press
Minneapolis, MN

Copyright © 2008 by Michael Arnold. All rights reserved.

Mill City Press, Inc.
212 3rd Avenue North, Suite 570
Minneapolis, MN 55401
612.455.2294
www.millcitypublishing.com

All rights reserved. No part of this publication may be reproduced, stored in a retrieval system, or transmitted, in any form or by any means, electronic, mechanical, photocopying, recording, or otherwise, without the written prior permission of the author.

ISBN - 978-1-934937-52-5
ISBN - 1-934937-52-5
LCCN - 2008942511

Cover Design and Typeset by Sophie Chi

Printed in the United States of America

miLLCITY
PRESS

To God: Thank you for the gift to write and the mind to not give up on it.

To my mom: I hung in there; this is the fruit of my labor. Let's reap together.

To Yemi: You were right. I would rather die trying than not try at all.

To my two sons, three nephews, and two nieces: you are the future of my groundwork—entrepreneurship.

For all of those who believe there is a better way and the nine-to-five isn't going to cut it anymore: this is for you.

Something that we must learn and establish upon the table of our heart is that Legacy is the expression of Entrepreneurship.

Michael Arnold

"There's something greater inside you; don't give up on it by staying on this job."

Yemi

"You're not stuck—your destiny is just that great."

Pastor Murphy

"The "afflatus moment" of one's life is when he becomes inspired to do what seems to be abnormal to someone else after he has first accepted the opportunity to do so."

Michael Arnold

"A memory that I always keep in mind is the fact that the system is always one up on us. They have laws, power, ability, and most of all money. Out of those four, I believe that everyone has the ability to overcome the first two and gain the latter."

Michael Arnold

"It would be a disheartening thing when I get to be fifty or sixty years old and my two sons ask me what I did that was so great in life."

Michael Arnold

INTRODUCTION

I never thought that I could ever reach a state in my mind where the world I know is like a systematic format that has been around since the days of creation. I can't fathom the thought that many of us will use it until the day that we die. That's right: until the day that we die. Without saying, there are a lot more credible things to die for such as your mother, son, wife, other family members, and or perhaps your car, house, or a clothing line that you faithfully buy when time allows. This system is so approved by the majority of us that some will find my accusation against this system to be cruel or unkind. This system that I speak of is none other then the nine-to-five work environment that the bulk of the earth's population is a part of. When you think about the word "system," probably the first thing that comes to mind is doing the same thing the same way all the time. One definition of system is "an organized set of doctrines, ideas, or principles usually intended to explain the arrangement or working of a systematic whole." Another meaning for the word "system," according to Random House dictionary, is "an organized or established procedure," and "systematic whole." These are words that I have lived by since the day that I started working.

It was very complicated for me to develop my own life and wants on a daily bases due to this established procedure and systematic whole. No matter how much I wanted to lay out of work, I found that almost impossible. Most people who don't like their jobs quit after a certain time working there. But as I got older, I realized that quitting wasn't the answer when I had a mandatory responsibility that calls for money. What would I do, how will I get past this fusion of bad actions that overshadows me like a horrific thought? These are thoughts that I struggled with for a long time in life.

I can't understand how a person can give their all to a job, giving years and years of consistently working for a company, and then out of the blue you're fired, laid off, the company is downsizing, or the job is moving out of the state—or what about this one: your services are not needed anymore. To me, it is absolute madness to hear anyone of these phrases come out of an employer's mouth. I hear people say this is just the way of life; you have to work. Bills have to be paid, my family has to eat. You work until you find something better. That's how the earth operates, period. "Really?" I asked myself this over and over again, saying, "there is a better way than this and it is tied to a moment, you will see."

Part 1

CHAPTER 1

A Look into the System

There are two main factions that make up the system: the owner and the employee. The two hold a distinct position in what I am calling the system. I have firsthand experience, understanding, and knowledge concerning how both parties work. The owner has the stance of owning the business, while the employee has the great job of making the owner's immense creation work to a tee. How do you do this? You wake up in the morning or at night if you're working that cruel and upsetting third shift, and you go and work on that job until your eight hours are up. Now, I don't know about you, but I hate that. Really, I don't like getting up in the morning or at night (I've done both) and going to a job and working forever and what seems like an eternity.

I have never in my life seen so many diverse jobs that are out there for people; from jobs that pay the most money to others that pay the lowest amount. I have only been on the low end of the payroll. Most jobs that are out there are designed to generate something, whether it's more money, more product, more employees, or just more time.

Whatever they generate, these jobs are systematically enforcing a plan by the owner that will implement his or her will ultimately on the employee. I admit this is a great marketing scheme for those that are in a position to do this as the owner. Those of us that are not, like myself, settle for working in an environment that we don't like or just don't want to be in at a certain time of the day or night. Why do we do this? One reason is money, another reason is for rank in the company, and others work just out of habit. This is a long and drawn-out system that has assisted us in these needs. The job force has been part of our lives for decades and will always be a part of our lives until we change that assertion. I remember working for a company many years ago. The company is a mega-force in society by far. I was married at the time and the job meant everything to me even though I was only making eight dollars an hour.

That's not much at all, I understand that, but when you're working and you're earning an income, it means something to a person that wants to pay bills and accept responsibility for his family. Previously I've been dismissed from jobs, but not without cause. For sake of time, I won't go deeply into the whole story of my getting fired. Basically, I was fired from that job because the employer believed that I wasn't doing what the job requirement requested and they said I violated a company rule. Was it true? Of course not! The company that hired the supervisor had given him or her the right to do this. They were downsizing and to make this effective, I was one of the ones who had to go.

This isn't anything new. This isn't the work of an evil person that's just out to get me because of my race, sex, height, or anything of the sort. Sometimes that may be the case, but in most instances, termination is brought on for a reason outside of what I just named.

I couldn't bear the mere thought of working for a company for almost seven years, the overtime hours that accumulated in that six-and-a-half-year time, busting my hind part, and then being terminated yet again. On this particular job, I was terminated for bringing a thumb drive to work. This may not have been serious to me, but it was serious to those who supervised me.

Now, in the report it stated that I violated a rule of the company. Feeling like I should have had less of a penalty didn't matter, because the rules for the job that I worked for were set in place. There isn't any way to change a rule that has been established and enforced by a supervisor, who is in essence an employee as well, but is also endorsed by the owner of the company. As an employee for six and a half years, what I failed to realized was that the system is clever. A word that I learned from a video game at twenty-four years old told me what the system thinks of me and my work ethic: it thinks I'm expendable.

It was my favorite video game during that time: Syphon Filter, a game that hooked me totally. In one part of the video game, the commander and chief of the evil regime told his man in charge to kill everyone on the ground who works for him. The word he used was expendable; a word that off the top of my head means replaceable. Wow, replaced, a substitute. I was one that could be swapped out for another. That's not a very good feeling to have to endure. Working in the system, you and I are just like the ground people that work for the commander and chief of my addictive game We are expendable, therefore the days at our job are numbered.

The idea of me being expendable didn't dawn on me until I was terminated in October of 2007, and by then it was too late; the damage had already been done. The owner of his establishment knows what it takes to make his creation work. It isn't a wonder that he or she is on top of the world and you and I are like the bum that eats crumbs from his master table. For some of us that's ok, eating crumbs from the master tables, but for me I don't want a little, I want the whole plate of food. The system has a personal agenda that it goes by, and it doesn't verbally express it amongst his employees.

It's a hidden secret that it speaks of daily among its own kind.

That secret is called wealth. That's something that the system generates on a daily basis. Let's get something clear, out in the open—we're just talking, so I can speak what's on my mind right? Thank you!

As of December fifteenth, 2007 (the second day into this project), wealth was a word that I knew nothing about but heard of through reading and seeing businesses and people of great resources. Charlotte, North

Carolina, a city known for its massive banking centers in the United States (number two to New York), knows what wealth is all about. Robert Johnson, founder of BET and the newly built Bobcats arena, has a close-knit relationship with wealth. J.K Rowling, with her Harry Potter books, has generated a land of milk and honey. Oprah Winfrey's magazine, called the "O" Magazine, produces so much wealth that I could take what her magazine makes in a year, and never have to work ever again in my lifetime.

Can you imagine the conversation that these big money-making systems are having with each other? Like people hang out with like people. Don't be fooled by what you hear. You may see nose-to-nose competitors like Pepsi and Coke or McDonalds and Wendy's go at it for the number one spot, but one thing is true: so much wealth runs through those four companies you will be seeing money signs for days. This isn't just true with the systems of big-time industries like McDonalds or Pepsi, but also with the church circuit. Yeah, that's right, I said the church! They make money too.

I read a report on Forbes.com that said there are billions of followers connected with the church. When you divide that up geographically from state-to-state and city-to-city, some of these bigger churches contain anywhere from fifteen thousand members to about thirty-five thousand and more.

Now, from a financial perspective, if each Sunday fifteen thousand members give ten dollars, then that's one hundred and fifty thousand dollars a Sunday! We won't even mention if we figure in a year of income, or if the membership is more than fifteen thousand. So it's clear to see that this system also is one that I would call a system of wealth. Systems that generate wealth prosper, thriving on what the employees do and not what the owners do.

The owners are overseers that put people in place to work the employees; so to speak, making sure that wealth is generated on a timely basis. What does the system's wealth have in common with the employees? Zero; nothing! So if we think that the owners like us so well, we are being deceived. They will do just enough to keep us there.

Jobs have programs that I will call "keeping the employee happy" programs. Some of them have 401Ks, social security, bonuses, vacation pay, holiday pay, and overtime pay.

These are just a few of the ways employees think they will benefit from the system. But as time would have it, we don't—the system benefits from us. I spoke with a friend that I talk to on a regular basis and we spoke about my recent termination. She is a real estate agent, which is a good job in my book depending on how many houses you sell and what your reputation is for selling houses. I don't know how many years she has been employed by her agency and how much she gets paid, but apparently it's not enough because she is a part-time teacher as well on the side. The conversation went as follows:

"How was work today, Mike?"

"I thought I told you, I don't work anymore." I said.

Her voice changed dramatically, and she blurted out the first words that came to her mind: "So you're not working any more?"

"Nope, I was tired of that job anyway."

"Well, you know you have bills to pay, so you're going to have to find something fast."

"I have a plan that I think will work, so in the meantime that's what I think I'm going to do to get it started."

She got quiet. If I didn't know any better, I would have thought she had seen a ghost or heard one at least. The moment I thought about the distance we had in our belief concerning the system, I realized how isolated I was and how devoted she is to functioning on a day-to-day basis in and through what I call the system.

Self-worth and wealth should go hand and hand, but through further observation and study you come to the conclusion that this is far from the truth. If an employee is working consistently on a job, starting and completing all of his duties, then in my eyes his self-worth is not very high. (But who am I?)

They say the more you know the better you are, but not exactly.

The system doesn't give you security. We advance and move up on jobs based on what we know but at anytime there is no reason why they will withhold letting you go That's why we train people for our job, then lose it to the one we trained that next week.

A person told me when I started at a security company in March of 2001 something that made a whole lot of sense. "So I see they hired you too."

"Yeah, I got the job. I thank God because I didn't have a job for a long time before I came here," I said loudly. My spirits were high. I smiled from ear to ear showing all my teeth. He then gazed at me like I had lost my mind. I knew he wanted to say "stop smiling, it's not that great," and in a sense that was exactly what he was saying.

"Have you ever done security, young man?" he asked, gazing hard at me in that cold training room that morning.

"No, but I can't wait to start." I kept wondering why this short, heavy-set, olive-skinned man was so disturbed about me liking the idea that I would be working security.

Then I finally got an answer for my longing thought.

"There is no security in security. You can work your ass off for three long months and then be fired the next day." I looked at him strangely, when suddenly the smile left my face. "You never worked security before, so they'll break you in slowly."

"I'm just working for the insurance. If they get on my nerves too badly, I'll quit on their asses and they won't see me the next day."

I still remember the last words he said like my first taste of vanilla ice cream with nuts and a bit of banana in it. (Man that's good!) "They don't pay you for what you're really worth, young man. They'll sidetrack your ass, but you'll see what I am talking about."

I never forgot those words, and I never thought that almost seven years later I would be in agreement with him. I never had the opportunity to work with him, but if I had, I could only imagine what would have taken place with all the setbacks and other things that went on at the job.

I think it's safe for me to say that these systems (jobs) never pay us what we're really worth. No matter how we complain about a greater work obligation, twelve-hour shifts, six- or sometimes seven-day work-weeks, working someone's shift—it doesn't work at all when you're speaking of your self-worth. All of us that worked on a job will admit that to be the truth whether we want to or not. Self-worth is important and jobs know this—that's why in most cases they get the best candidates for the job, not someone who will be willing to work the position no matter what.

In acquiring those candidates (you and I), they demand what you and I will do or else they will find another candidate. I'm not saying that we should call our own shots, dictate what we will and won't do, but I think it's an idea that should be considered first before tossing it completely out the window. A job makes us inferior to the real world, the outside box, the part of the world that says it knows something that the system isn't telling me.

What is it? It isn't a good thing to me, to be placed in a position that gives you no choice other than to work accordingly or hit the highway. Some may think that this form of philosophy is not that cut-and-dried. Try this: next time you apply for a job and you really feel that you want to work there, after filling out the job application and they hire you, tell them every one of your dos and don't that you want to implement before you start and see what happens.

The fact of the matter is that we are the lowest of low on the totem poll, not because we aren't knowledgeable enough, but because the system has all the control, all the power, and all the authority. Positions do come and go, but for those that own the system, that's far from being the case. As for you and me, well, we may experience money here and money there, but never at a level that the owners do.

Now the big question comes to mind: how do we change this? Many have found an answer, and for years have gone on in the system never seeing that answer to be that of real truth and instead finding more anger, more frustration and most of all a lot of pain going forward.

CHAPTER 2

Finding a Needle in a Haystack

As little children playing on the floor of the living room or perhaps in the loneliness of our bedrooms, we thought of dreams that somehow always seemed to make those moments as dreaming children that much more interesting. No, it wasn't that our parents would come in and hug us, speaking words that gave us notice that they love us. It wasn't that time when we got to eat the last piece of chocolate cake because we finished all of our dinner. It was those dreams, those enlightening things that brought us the most joy when we were youth.

We would dream in the comfort of our own world as we saw it, not as anyone else may have perceived it to be, but as we viewed it. Those dreams that were formatted and brought out in the open were all we had. Then we grew, not only in a physical form, but mentally as well, seeing those same dreams again, only this time vaguely because the reality has set in. We were grown men and women with responsibilities that had been so riveted in our mind that we tossed those dreams aside for the reality of stronger responsibilities.

That may be all right to a number of you, but to those of us who still dream and have dreams from just that moment from childhood, our adult responsibilities aren't enough. We see more, therefore we want more, and our dreams continue on even as young men and women, elderly veterans in the race of life who will not relinquish life until that dream is walking hand and hand with them until the end and the beginning of their eternal life.

I found myself thinking of some dream, some connection that would see me past the system after looking into it from a depth perspective. The Bible says, "and with all thy getting get an understanding." Regardless of a pending belief in the Bible, it makes a whole lot of sense to me.

A lot of us work the system, believe in the system, represent the system, and spend most of our lives in the system. In the last chapter we found the system to be that of a burden more than a liberation era that all of us deserve. I don't think anyone reading this book wants to be pestered by a person sitting behind an oak green desk, a computer in front of them, a fuming attitude to go along with the desk and computer, hoping to take back your car if you show any sign of a late payment.

A mortgage, rent, car payment and credit card, to say the least, happen to irritate in more ways than one when you see or hear of millionaires spending thousands upon thousands of dollars on clothing apparel, cars and other accessories they buy without a credit card. Please don't mention the long, costly trips that they take and lavish in for no other reason but that they have the freedom to do so. We marvel at the fact that the house we live in is a two-hundred-thousand-dollar house, and the car that we drive is a fifty-thousand-dollar car that we often times admire from our bedroom window.

Our cell phone isn't just a cell phone but also a computer, giving complete access to the Internet. I would be holding out on you if I neglected the fact that those same cell phones also have a camera built into the memory base, giving you a one-finger press that will activate the camera from anywhere.

The sentiment we get when we think about all of these things is what we call somewhat of a blessing, success on a high level, while those who don't have any of the above features are just unsuccessful nincompoops. We fail to realize that those who buy cars or houses actually *buy* those cars and houses. There isn't any disclaimer or requirement of the sort that bars them from *buying* anything. In the past my getting has been just that, without understanding but with madness and obligation.

Credit, cars, and more jobs have been my understanding for years, in order to keep the credits cards, cars, and whatever else I found to get in debt for. We compare ourselves to each other only to realize that in comparison we both come out the same, with no clear-cut difference. The challenge isn't to find a higher position in the most successful system in our area (or anywhere for that matter), but to be the most successful person in a position to own the successful system.

From a one-on-one viewpoint, that's easier said than done; it's like finding a needle in a haystack. A question may arise that asks: if you lose a needle, why would you look for it? You would be better off just getting a new one. That would be true only if that wasn't grandma's favorite needle, and if she weren't expecting it back in the next hour. But rather than look for the needle we feel that every needle is the same, so we go purchase another thinking it's the same, but in all actuality it's not—it's different. The conversation that people have with me is kind of one sided. People normally talk and I just listen, unless I have a good point to make that will help the both of us. I have a low tolerance for the same old dull dry conversation that goes nowhere, so instead of getting angry, we both view the topic, make our point, then go our separate ways.

A lady that goes to my church talks to me occasionally about different things such as church topics, her former living condition in her formal residents, her divorce, and more than anything; her job teaching. Of course she talked negatively about her job, explaining to me in detail how she feels that they are trying hard to keep a high position away from her.

I waited to see if her end of the conversation would change. I must admit it did change, turning into her thoughts of moving somewhere else in search of a new job.

Don't get me wrong, I enjoyed speaking to her (I always do), but nothing in that conversation said things would be better for her. Just like her conversation and many others I indulged in, a question arises in my mind more so than any other. That question is, "What are you doing so differently from everyone else that one day will possibly make a difference, not just in my life, but someone else's life as well?" There are a few people like this in the world, and most of the time they turn out to be one of the greatest, if not the greatest, that the world has ever seen in their time and in times to come.

As I go almost into my third month of unemployment, I firmly realize that just finding another job is realistic, but not ideal for me. Not you, but someone you know, might say, "That man is crazy; where did he get that belief from?" That's OK. Opinions and comments are welcome, that's not a problem, but I will explain myself so the next time you see them you can relay the message that I didn't leave anything out.

In the process of my writing two unpublished manuscripts (this being the third one) I have the strong belief, since being rejected by publishers a total of twenty or more times, that there is a slim hope for change. Writing is my pride and joy; I have to contain it, then bring it forth—my idea that one day someone will finally read this pride and joy of words and think it makes some sense. That, in my terms of thoughts, is a great ideal. I could take the normal route that everyone else takes, and believe that the system will work for me when in fact it didn't do anything for me in the past. That's being realistic. Those of us who are realistic sometime never make the grade in people's eyes. We are considered strange and even dumb.

Then you have others that never move up to where their hearts want them and so they develop a productive activity only within the system and not in life. How many times do we use something many times, whether it's good or bad, and we look for a different result only to find the same one?

I understand that the system will only give you what you have been giving, that's all. So that's why we fall behind in our bills, have car payments and mortgage payments that extend higher than the sky, and credit card expenses that we are not happy about but will continue to charge in the name of our good credit thinking that somehow our max out credit card will suddenly have a zero balance .

It is only a handfulof society that are in control over themselves versus being controlled by someone or something. I have yet to find the positive aspect of car payments, overwhelming credit card payment, rent and mortgage which is the essence of what we live for. But where are the people that believe the "Needle in the Hay Stack" mentality? Yes it is very true that credit is good and it appears to be the solution for the No Cash Syndrome, but what happens if the charging of merchandise takes over all that we do making that the attraction of existence? Irretrievable action then becomes a reality.

We snarl at the mistake that we made in getting into a mortgage that we can't pay. Instead of buying enough to survive we buy more than we can handle. We want people to understand what we are going through. They may have a strong act of disbelief, but the fact still remains: if you're not doing anything contrary to getting free from the system, then basically you're not doing anything to advance yourself. They say that there are two different paths to where you want to go in life: the straight and narrow path, or the crocked and wide path. But within the straight and narrow path, there arc signs that help you along the way. One sign is knowing that the needle-in-the-haystack mentality should mean more to us then a system mentality.

Have you just taken the time to not just turn on your TV, but actually observe what is being broadcasted upon our airwaves? Not that it's so much sex, violence, and more food shows than you can think of, but have you seen the number of shows that compete with each other? For the Oprah show you have The Tyra Show, for The Young And The Restless you have All My Children, so on and so forth. I am very much aware that these people and companies make thousands and even millions per year, but is that all? Isn't that why we are so attached to the system anyway—because of money? Is that why the outcome of our lives is a demand by the system instead of ourselves? We say "there" in answer, but we tarry by the wayside, never becoming the rare few that are hard to detect. Every one of these people decide a long time ago that they wanted to be rare, not having a mortgage, buying a car straight out instead of having a car payment, paying all their bills and not having to pay the bill last month this month.

They decided that those dreams that they had would turn into strategy and the strategy brings about those who are the few, the rare and those that are finding a needle in a haystack.

CHAPTER 3

Who We Really Are

I never saw my father except for one time in my life, and I had to be about three or four years old. The brief meeting was so vague that if he walked past me in an empty Wal-Mart shopping center I still couldn't tell you who he was. I have heard from pastors, televisions shows, and many parenting programs that say that a child will struggle in childhood and even into adulthood without a father in his life.

I didn't know that, sitting in the living room floor playing by myself, enjoying the moment, loving my early days as a child. Back then all I really was was a kid that didn't have a problem having all the fun that a child could have, all by his lonesome. Friends in my neighborhood came over and we had a ball playing with our toys and just enjoying childhood. (Not like children now; they are different, but that's another story.)

Most of the time, creating a world of my own seemed to generate more of an excitement than having my friends over that I saw occasionally. It wasn't that I despise their company, trust me—as many things as I had to do around the house, I took advantage of every moment that my community friends and I could create recreation amongst ourselves. They meant the world to me, and I knew I meant the world to them.

Meaning the world to someone doesn't negate the fact that I am still my own unique person regardless if that someone is there or not. My entire mental makeup as a child was that of an isolated one that hinged strongly upon creativity, which was inspired by my own toys. I didn't have any trouble fixing or making things work from my own mind hey that what most kids done when I was a child.

My friends developed a huge amount of credibility in making those dreams come true during our playtime. I ask myself questions on a daily basis, and if I knew the answer then I would give myself a reply. (No, I'm not crazy—just exploring my thought process.) One of those questions that I asked came from statements people made concerning another person. Here's one: "In order to find success for yourself you have to have a successful person in your life. Your success depends on another person. If you don't do what I tell you to do, then you will fail…"

I'm going to stop right here. Just typing these statements in my computer is starting to get under my skin. Undoubtedly I missed some major time with not having my father in my life and he has missed some extraordinary moments in my life. But does it really matter? Life still goes on and with a mother like mine…. she did a great job in raising me. I just didn't take heed to some of her suggestions for my adulthood life.

In life, I made some decisions that weren't great, so I won't repeat them here. But overall, I knew who I really was. The more time we spend working in a nine-to-five atmosphere, the less we know who we are from the inside out in our personal lives. There isn't a remedy out there that can change the way you are created. Contrary to popular belief, we may choose to alter our physical genders or change our appearances, but we are who God created us to be, period.

For instance, I am a writer. That's my passion. I love to write as long as my fingers will allow me to. It's something that isn't a requirement, but an opportunity to perform what is already in me. There are two abilities that I don't have but wish I did, and those are singing and drawing. Those are two expressions that are probably a shorter-term project than the writing expression. I heard people make the argument that you can learn anything that you want, to which I partially agree. Where there's money there's a way, so yes, in a sense they're right. But if you don't have the passion and the drive it's money wasted.

I feel that if it's not already in you, then it may be complicated to exercise it at all times. Many singers, actors and actress, painters, and sport figures—not all, but some—have a embedded desire to not just accomplish something in their passion, but to become who they already are in it. That means that it is their existence. They breathe it as if their lives depended on it.

Before I began to write this morning, I counted again how many times I have been rejected by big-name literary agencies. The reason I do this is to always remind myself that those seventeen companies rejected me only based on their decisions, not the whole entire publishing world's. Not one time in writing anything did I feel as though I wouldn't get published. It's only when we know who we are not that the fear comes. My mom didn't tell me much about my father except that he wasn't there.

By no means, do I believe that her time spent with him wasn't important at first, before he decided to cut out based on the type of person my mother is. A couple of friends that were close to me in my younger years asked me if I missed not having a father. I wanted to say in a loud, bold scream, "A WHO??" I quickly changed my mind to avoid all thoughts on their part of me being totally deranged and crazy.

In all spirit I may have sounded foolish, but in all honesty I would have been right on point with that outburst. I learned a long time ago in my younger years (Although I'm not that old), just because you have the title to be or do something doesn't make you whatever it is.

My father has the title of a father because he helped create me, but he doesn't have the heart of one. When he walked out of my life, not out of the relationship with my mom, but out of my life, that's when he said to himself that he doesn't want to be a father.

No one in the world has to tell him that he has kids. I'm pretty sure he knows that. But maybe someone should have told him how to be a father.

Early on in my adulthood I felt like kids were the biggest headache one man could have in his blessed life. It was like having a pain in my head that I couldn't get rid of even after taken an aspirin. They were everlasting to me— would they just *go*! I couldn't function when they were around. I walked out of the room hoping they would shut up when they no longer saw me there. What I couldn't understand (in all thy getting, get an understanding) was that I didn't like who I really was in the inside and that was a child.

I couldn't hate the one that had a part in my physical birth but didn't have a part in who I really am—his biological son. So to all of those that are reading this that grew up as my childhood friend, the answer I have now is no, I'm not mad I don't have my father in my life. You can't be anything that you really don't have in your heart and with him he just didn't want that responsibility.

For almost seven years I work, labored, and battled in a place I didn't want to be. For months, years, and sometimes for all of our lives we compromise who we are for the system in order to make a dollar. The question I should ask isn't about compromising but who we really are. In the world of the job age, it's more about them than you. It's more about money in their hand and more in their bank account.

That's all well and fine on their behalf. They created their separate world that they benefit monetarily from, and that's expected from a mind that knows how to generate money. We usually are the people that circulate money in and out of the system for the owner. For example, in working many years for million dollar companies, I've heard a lot. Normally when your ears are open, you tend to hear the negative about something more than the positive.

When I started working for security in 2001, I thought it was the best thing since sliced bread. By far, it was the easiest job I ever had in my life and I cherished it more than I cherished time away from that place. The site that I worked at for five years (downtown Charlotte,

North Carolina) gave me rest and it gave me money. The rest that I received from working security came when I was able to do the job that was required of me while sitting on my butt. The money came every other week at no stress whatsoever.

It came so much and so fast through overtime I had adopted the nickname, "Iron-man" by my security director. It was a draining period of my life leading into about the third year of working there even with the "Iron-man" title.

The nickname was ok, but it wasn't who I was. The money was fabulous all around the board. If they didn't know me by "Iron-man," my co-workers knew I had a plan to make more money than I was making on just my forty-hours-a-week check.

The most I ever worked was about 160 hours within a two-week time span and my check was about sixteen thousand dollars for those two weeks. "Boy I bet you killed them this week on that check, didn't you Mike?" a co-worker asked, waiting on me to open up with the information.

"You know I worked all the overtime—I killed them!" I couldn't explain how excited I was to have not only a check like that at my disposal and on top of that cashing it.

That excitement would soon turn into disappointment after it was all spent on bills. It wasn't hard for me to figure that in order for me to have this kind of money every pay check, as I started to expect, then I was going to have to work myself like a dog just by showing up for work everyday.

That year (2001) people complained about incomplete checks, checks that didn't have employees' full pay amount, but instead a lower amount that wasn't close to overtime pay.

This was always happening when employees like myself worked a lot of hours. Finally, after talking to a few coworkers about their pay, we all found out when we didn't received that yearly raise that we expected, and that the security company, who made that easy job feel like we were working in the coal mines, was charging their client forty dollars an hour for each security officer and paying us $10.38 an hour.

That fact didn't dawn on me at all until days, month, and years passed and none of us were benefiting from our work when we didn't see an increase in pay. The money of course didn't cut it. It generated from the bottom all the way to the top and it didn't decline.

I had every reason to change my perspective on the way we were looked at on this job. It's sad to say, but all of us, from the supervisor down, were drones. No matter how much we thought that forty dollars over ten dollars was bad, there wasn't anything we could do until we thought differently about ourselves.

The supervisors of that day weren't any better—they only received a couple dollars more an hour for a difficult task that should have paid them fifteen dollars an hour. Meetings were held on a regular basis and we were getting our hopes up thinking we might get a pay raise. But they were all bogus meetings to let us know that they are still in control. We look at time in the forties, fifties and sixties, and we ask ourselves (some of us), how can one person rule over another person in such a way that he doesn't have any control of himself?

It's hard to digest that thought (for me anyway) and our conclusion to that question is: I would never do that. I would never allow anyone to have that much power over me. Do they know who I am? I am not the one; they better think again.

I can say that honestly and wholeheartedly, because I said those words and I believed those words. There wasn't a soul out there that could tell me that I was going to be ruled by someone sitting on his ass (excuse my language) in a front office and demanding what I'm going to do and what I'm not going to do. The more I said that to myself, the more I found myself doing it.

It's not a good feeling to know that I didn't have an identity. A distinctiveness that reflects on something other than devotion to a company, who didn't give a damn about me, where I wanted to go, and how I would get there, or if I would ever get there. Knowing where I was going is like me being brainless: I didn't have a clue.

One thing that I know now is that whatever is inside you has to be equivalent to what's in your mind and heart. What's in your heart and mind has to be like a husband and wife, a hand and a glove. Like a business.

More times than one our hearts tell us who we really are, but because there isn't a visual, our mind tells us what we can actually see and comprehend. What our mind does is capture the situation, remember it, and relive it over and over again, forming a conclusion until it has persuaded the heart by overwhelming confidence that what the mind has said is the truth.

The suffering is only the long-term process, but the short-term process of this is that the heart has a stronger battle overcoming the mind, trying to get it back in harmony with overcoming that negative condition. I have read a few books, heard from a couple of people in all sorts of venues, and what have I heard? All sorts of solutions. One solution that I learned in all of this is finding out who I really am. One way I have done this is discovering my passion for life and why God placed me on this earth. Contrary to what people have said, they don't make that decision for you. No one tells you what your passion in life is. Only God will give you the answer to that question.

They might be able to help, and that's a big "might," depending on who that person is.

When you realize that there is something inside of you like I did, and it continues to tell you that there is more to life than just making $10.38 an hour, you can become something in life that will allow you to go to the doctor and dentist whenever you need to and not worry about how you am going to pay for the treatment. That's the life God wants for all of us.

My life won't be a life where someone else tells me when to wake up, when to go to sleep, how much money I will make, when I will go home, and most of all, the one I heard more than any of these, "Thank you, Mr. Arnold, but your services are no longer needed." (Well, they weren't that sentimental, but you know what I mean) Your heart will speak of things that pertain to you and who you really are.

I remember just about six months or so from my starting this manuscript, I worked at a company for three years unloading one airplane. The job became an instant favorite of mine. It brought out the man in you if you were a little introverted in the work duties.

That's the one and only job that I can and will say that those guys were like family to me. One of those guys inspired me more than he knew. I would always debate my beliefs; making my points known to everyone there. They thought I was stupid and a little extreme with some of the things I said and actually believed.

After all of it was over, our battles ended in peace, no hard feelings. But there is one thing that I remember from my coworker James that is so vital to me now. "Mike, let me holler at you man!" He said. To be honest, I didn't want to hear anything James or anyone else working for the airlines had to say. I felt strongly that what they were saying was hurting me, and they didn't see what I saw.

"What, James?" I said waiting on the verbal cutting from him that I knew he was going to give me.

"I know it sounds like we're picking on you, but we're not. We just don't want you to make the same mistakes we made."

The conversation from his end seemed to be more sincere than normal, so I focused on his words. I felt like I was in the midst of a trial and the guys that worked with me were the jury. "We're old men Mike, and we've already been through what you're going through. We might not be right all the time and you don't have to agree with us either, but everything we say you don't have to debate all the time, man!"

I listened word by word as James continued to talk. He gave little room for anyone else to speak or have their chance to take me down verbally. "You know what I do, man?" I didn't respond, I just let him tell me. "I listen to what people tell me, but I don't have to agree with them. You use your ears to filter out what you don't agree with; you don't have to debate with everyone." That made sense. I didn't dispute it, I didn't find fault in those words; instead, I embraced them and held on to them like they were my life. To this day I believe that James is one of the few people that believed in me.

Not that I depended on his or anyone else's words as a means of getting somewhere, but just to know that someone is in your corner who does believe in you does make you smile every once in a while.

James and I had many conversations before and after this one. He would always tell me that he thought that I was a good person and I was trying to do better. James believed in me and I believed in his words. His words confirmed the ultimate word that God said about me a long time ago.

The mistakes I made on that job and everywhere else didn't indicate that I was a bad person, but it showed clearly that I was a human being. Mistakes, I believe, only show the growing process of your life, but the heart shows you who you really are after those mistakes have been made and corrected.

Deep down in my heart I want to own a house, a motorcycle, help all who I can help to reach their destiny in life (family and friends), and most of all be an inspiration to anyone who will listen to me.

Thoughts of that coming to pass has to be gained only in the imagination first, then delivered in an arena where I will be willing to receive it. Not too many people want to hear what you want to do outside of that job—if you don't believe me, next time you're on your job, try it.

Go up to one of your coworkers (not just anyone, one that you have conversations with the most) and just begin to tell that person your biggest dream in the world and see what their response will be. Now, they may be for you at first, but I guarantee you that if that is the source of your conversation everyday they are going to get tired of it unless they too are hoping to dream big and get away from the nine-to-five system one day with you.

The reason I speak of this is that I find so many times that people don't know who they are, and somewhere down the line they don't want you to discover who you are either. During this time of not having any income, my mind told me plainly I have to find some sort of income until I get published. I went everywhere my grey Chevy Cavalier would take me until I finally found a place that would hire me.

"Yes, this company is hiring. Are you interested in working for us?"

Hell, no is what I thought, but I answered appropriately: "Yeah, I'm interested in working, but what is the pay, sir?"

"Well, this security company only pays eight dollars an hour, but we have a lot of hours for you if you want it, Mr. Arnold." He said smiling as big as the sky.

I thought, *you've got to be kidding me—hours like that aren't something to smile about,* but I didn't want to pass on this sure opportunity to work again.

I filled out the application and I was all set to work. "Mr. Arnold, I have a small question for you before we start your processing." I'm thinking, *what now, it's already bad that the job is $8.00 dollars an hour. What else could be wrong?* "How attached are you to that beard?"

I looked somewhat curiously, but knew exactly what he meant. "I can't shave my beard completely off, but I can shave it down."

"OK, sounds good; get it shaved as low as it will go without shaving it off, and we will see you in the morning around one." Between that evening and the next I went through all different type of changes only to hear the next morning, "Mr. Arnold, we need that beard completely off before we can process you for this job."

CHAPTER 4

Faith is the Mechanism

I couldn't believe what I was hearing. Did this security guard really know who I was? "I just spoke with the major (the head of the security company), and he said that your beard isn't going to cut it. You will have to shave it completely off before we can process you for this job."

To be truthful, a bad feeling came over me like a shadow. A small cage-like covering surrounded me and I felt as though I was standing before a judge pleading my case (again). I walked out of that office, thought about what had just taken place, and walked back inside. "Why didn't you tell me that you wanted me to shave my beard completely off before I drove forty-five minutes over here and waited on my barber to shave me, only to hear you say that you won't accept this!"

I know who I am; this one moment declared that I wasn't going to stand before someone who doesn't care about me and where I was going. In essence I guess I was standing before a judge. "Mr. Arnold, I thought we made that clear to you over the phone yesterday evening."

"What you made clear over the phone and also in person was that I will shave it down—that's what you told me!"

"I'm sorry, Mr. Arnold."

Realizing who you really are is the first step to recovery. The second step is using a little something that's going to get who you are in the face of other people. And for me it's faith. I'm not stupid, I may not know much as many do that walk with a college degree in their front pocket, but I do have common sense and I knew I could do better with this job situation than I was doing.

Money is important and with money you have all the capabilities of paying your bills and with a job you can do that. But after all the bills are paid and there is nothing left, what are you going to do? This question arose more times than one. And this time I wasn't going to look like a person who is desperate just to get a job to pay bills and that's it. My heart says that I'm a winner, that there is so much more inside of me that I can discover, and my mind is in agreement with that, so what's left to do?

"Have a good day, sir." Those words were his spears that he hoped would kill me, but his only target was a shield of faith. He didn't know that, but who cares, as long as I contained the belief that if all he had for me is an eight-dollar-an-hour job and a mind that says to me, "you either take it or leave it; this isn't a place where you can negotiate why you can't shave."

That may sound harsh and maybe arrogant to some, but to us, we could care less what they think or say. Our minds and our hearts are in communion with each other, and we are not going to let someone from the system break then destroy who we are. The pill I swallowed that evening could have been that of depression, sadness, a mind that wants to give up saying to myself there is no hope, the light at the end of the tunnel never has been there and is definitely not there now. That could have been that pill.

But what I swallowed was a pill of confidence, self-assurance in myself that hinged upon my heart and spoke volumes of assertions that things would be OK even if I didn't take that job. There was something working for me behind closed doors.

I am so tired of people never ceasing to speak on the things they have or what position that they hold. One thing about thinking is that you can always place your own conclusion to the conversation in your mind without arguing with them. (Thank you, James.) I have a hard time believing that I have so much belief that one day I will own a house, but I can't believe that I will have the funds to pay for it. Right now as we speak, December 24, 2007, a day before Christmas, my world is full of everything else but a positive outlook. Everything but the right thing is happening to me.

To be honest, it is more than difficult to smile in the face of adversity when you know that you are in the midst of the rug being pulled right from under you. It's easy to smile, walk around as if you're the ruler of the earth, when every bill in your house is paid for that month and everything is going good.

A car, a house, or even a job won't do it when you're faced with these challenges. Furthermore, when you know that you are better than that, it makes you angry. I don't know about you, but I don't have a problem concluding that faith is more important to me than being in debt to a car, a house, and a job.

Correct me if I'm wrong, but when you're on a job, you're paying time to that job that most people never pay off! Of course you get a check in exchange for this debt, but nowhere near what you're supposed to get paid (what you are really worth). But just like a house, you pay year after year after year and it never gets paid for until after thirty years into the mortgage. The system makes you think that if you get a better job than you can pay things off and have more financial freedom.

How am I free financially when my finances don't free me? With me recently going into debt to purchase a car, I am quickly finding out how much faith it has taken me to exercise, without any income, while the car company threatens to take my vehicle back during my hard times.

Once you get enough car dealership and bill collectors calling your house, then you will be able to put a finger on the notch that tells us where we really are in life. I learned quickly that if I wanted to be who my heart told me I was, I had to do much more than go in debt to get something that didn't even belong to me.

Speaking about hurt, I think I hurt more in a struggle exercising who I am now then hurting from a bodily injury of some type. There are hundreds, maybe thousands, of lifestyles that we conduct daily that cause us more grief than freedom. Part of a fruitful life for me is to establish a scheme that will carry me into something that I have never been a part of that in return will give me postivity.

Hurting is a part of the everyday life that we try to avoid by people and behavior that we think will override that hurt, but in the end we suffer from it anyway and we haven't learn anything.

I come to find out that learning for me is not necessary learning something new, but applying something I already know that I haven't been following that could nine times out of ten change my life. So for me it's not how good I got it because I have "things" but what plan will I come up with to pay it off?

A question that I ask myself many times that I will never stop asking, is: What do I have to do to change my situation? The answer I came up with flowed throughout my mind fluidly, like water running down from an open stream. It said to act on your heart's words that in return will change your circumstances and your life. I hear those words daily, especially when things in my life seem to go everywhere but the right way.

At first I didn't have a clue what that meant, until I thought on those words more and more each day. Growing up, I never knew that a person could overcome a trial that plagued them and their generation for years, and maybe all of their life. I thought whatever bad is going on in a person's life, then that's what they will forever have.

I just believed that a certain type of person owned businesses and those of us that grew up poor and unfortunate were the ones that had to work the rest of their lives, never coming out of that nine-to-five system. Very seldom did I hear people talk about life outside of what they were bound to. All I heard people talk about is getting the best job they can get to take care of their families and that's all.

No one ever talks about anything different. I heard people talk briefly about how I can become whatever I chose to be, but never explained how. No one ever explains how, as if becoming who you wanted to become is virtually impossible to explain. The more I came to grips with my thoughts, I was slowly realizing that what I imagined could actually come true (That was Faith in action and I didn't know it).

Without a shadow of a doubt, I knew that it would take a whole lot of something besides boldness to tell that security company weeks ago, "he can keep his job, I don't want it," knowing I didn't have a job. For me it took a strong dose of what is called faith. Seeing something happen that you want to happen goes against the majority.

Jobs to me are stepping stones, a bridge between ordinary and great, sought-after but not preferred by those who seek continuity. In my reference of thinking, it takes a little faith or perhaps no faith at all to hinge my life's success on an occupation that can open and close the door on the money I am allowed to make.

When you are among the job circuit and your bills depend on your money and the possibility of your not having enough, the faith factor comes into play only to make more money to cover your bills, but not to get out of the job circuit. That's how we want faith to work for us.

I have found more times than one that if faith is embraced on a serious and intimate level, like a marriage, then the outcome will be that of expectancy; that same expectancy that we just think on and never make it come to pass.

So how should this faith thing be handled? In my opinion, instead of attempting to use faith to try and get more money on a dead-end job, I use faith as a mechanism- a device to get me out of the job circuit period; not to just get a better job. (We have already done that and it has gotten us nowhere now let do something different).

Faith is like a long-time friend that for all the good reasons, we embrace because we have so much confidence in it. Faith is also like one of those other friends that at first you don't see any positive result from, but as time progress on and you keep watching and believing in them, then finally they give you that expectancy that you thought you would see in them.

Without faith working in one's life, it becomes difficult to get loose from this system, the mindset of disparity that comes from the everyday pressure of that day job will soon take over you life and faith will be like the wind here and gone in a instant. Sometimes I tend to stray away from faith only to find that without this close friend, this mechanism of a vent, I have come back to is like a wife that I walked out on, finally realizing after being without her, she is my all, and I need her more and more each day.

I think some of us so badly want to do away with our work in the system and come to grips with who we are that we sometimes do things that don't give faith a chance to operate and we bear the burden of the system and everything that comes along with it. For me, I am a work in progress, and so with every day that passes I want to give faith a chance to see something take place in my life that's never happened to me before.

I've seen firsthand what the system is all about, what comes out of it and what they allow me to receive from it. I never want to experience an eternal working lifestyle where I will never become who I'm supposed to be. With faith as a mechanism I won't ever have to worry about that.

CHAPTER 5

"All things are lawful unto me, but all things are not expedient: all things are lawful for me, but I will not be brought under the power of any." (1 Corinthians 6:12)

In search of that friend, that companion, the one that can open a door that has never been opened before, I realize that the system has been a consistent part of my life for the last sixteen or seventeen years. They say what you don't know won't hurt you, and I'm almost willing to believe that cliché if I don't get hurt.

During those sixteen to seventeen years I was never taught that faith could not only work for me, but also be my best friend. I wouldn't say that's the fault of someone else, but I will take blame for it.

Many of us have questions (at least I do) that pertain to our lives. We are like a huge puzzle that has not been completed yet, and all the pieces are scattered around in life's situation. With these life situations we come in contact with another puzzle piece that gets us closer to an answer for our life.

Many times in my own life I haven't been so eager to embrace those pieces that I find scattered around; instead I relinquish them like bad habits, finding my life incomplete containing holes and cracks that stall my life, placing me in bondage. Up until this point, bondage hasn't been a real joy for me, especially when I find it such a struggle to get out of that hold that has me backpedaling.

I strongly agree that after you put your feet in backward mode enough time, you will find (like me) that something has to change down the road if you're going to stop backpedaling and get out of the bondage crisis. I'm not that old; I'm still considered to be young (thank God!), so in my young life thus far, I have seen and experienced all sorts of bondage that has rested, ruled, and abided in my life.

I know all of us know precisely what I mean when I speak of bondage.

For the sake of those who don't know what I am referring to, I am simply speaking about the power that someone else has over your life. You don't have a complete say in your life.

For a period of time I thought it was OK for me to go to work, come home, eat, go to sleep, then do it all again the next morning. That's what I believed life should be for everyone that lives on earth. If that is what our thought persuaded us to believe, we are totally far off.

According to recent statistics for November 2007, the unemployed rate is at 4.7 percent. From my perspective, that is an astounding statistic. Round that off to 5 percent, and you have approximately 95 percent of people in the month of November employed.

Those 95 percent of people do not have a total say so in their life so at least 8 hours a day, they go to a job telling them how a job is suppose to be done, what time to get there, how much their pay rate will be, and the time they are dismissed from that job.

The message that is relayed to me mentally is that there are a lot of people that are employed somewhere in the earth. There are millions, to be exact. But how many of those millions have come to grips with the part of our lives that will get us thinking our way out of the job circuit, honestly realizing that it's bad working and even worst not doing anything about it?

When I was a young kid, maybe between four and twelve years, my mom told me a story of actuality after I told her words of impracticality.

The dialogue went something as follows:

"Michael, I thought I told you to get those toys out of that living room floor."

"I am, Mom."

"I guess you don't want them then, do you?" She didn't stutter; her words were strong, plain and to the point without any additives. "I told you now, not later. If you don't get those toys up, boy, I'll throw them away then we won't have to worry about them being in that floor. I'm not going to keep telling you this over and over again. I'm the boss in here not you."

I looked at my mom like she was stupid, but in all actuality stupidity showed widespread on my face more than on hers.

If I knew what I know now, instead of just allowing my toys to lie on the floor, I would have picked them up before my mom had made her declaration to me.

What my mom was insinuating all those years ago, just in case I didn't know, was that she enforced a law that I had to abide by daily, period. No questions asked. If I didn't know anything else, one thing that did rehearse in my mind was all of my mother's laws in that house didn't go unenforced.

She was the head of that household, and that's what was expected. It was lawful unto me to follow what held our house in order. Not only were the rules of the house lawful unto me, they were lawful for me.

Why was this a particular growing up? More than anything, these laws that my mom enforced for my sister and I showed that she is in control over the house and how it should be run, and she made sure we followed them or we suffered the consequences.

This isn't any different from the way your everyday job works. But more importantly, the consequences that we suffer at home aren't as nearly as tragic as working within the system. We might experience punishment all day after school in our room, but never a dismissal from our home.

But the mind of the system is ubiquitous, worldwide, and determined when it comes to their discipline. They don't associate feelings with their conclusion, but only a stingy rebuke that leaves those of us that work in this system powerless. Powerless to the fact that faith doesn't have a seat anywhere in a place that has power over us if we choose not to change it.

We are very impetuous when it comes to others dictating what will and what will not go on in each and every one of our lives. That theory is an approachable belief, seeing that most of us fight daily to keep others out of our personal affairs. So to be built in and around a system that doesn't allow that only means one thing: that our private lives are substituted by a law that requires us to work in spite of it.

Many may feel, whenever in need, apply a source that will supply that need. That sounds good, but not such a theory will bring a solution to a problem to one but many difficulties that never lead us out but keeps us locked down to its laws. During my years as a child and hearing all sort of things from my mother's mouth, I discovered that those words shaped what she wanted and what she desired for us as children.

She maintained that once we are out of her house the rules (laws) that she enforced would no longer be a post for us to stand at. The jobs that we work on today (most of them) are our standing post in society.

The only difference from my mother's laws and the established laws of the system is they don't want us to break away from them at any point in life. A woman that at this time I consider a particular person in my life speaks to me on a regular basis about her aggravating job.

She is to a worker who desires a higher position and increase in pay (don't we all) that seems to always fall through on a number of occasions. "Michael, you know my situation, you know they are trying to keep me here when there is a higher position for me. What shall I do?"

That was the gist of the conversation that I had with her. "You know how I feel concerning the nine-to-five."

"I know Mike, but I'm not there yet, so I just want your opinion."

"The only thing that I can tell you is to make your case known to them. What your qualifications are, time spent in your field, your consistency there, and that's it."

"Mike, I am so tired of the way they are treating me I wish I could quit."

Of course I shook my head and thought to myself, *The law of the system, here we go again.*

Since she means so much to me as a friend, I explained to her how much of an importance it is for me to overcome this syndrome of working that caused me to beat myself physically every single day for nothing.

I also told her how many years I hurt from this domineering system, this system of control, laws that only enable more currency to the owner and more stress for you and I in a long drawn-out work habit that leaves us with nothing. Did she bite on my experience and words of affirmation?

I think she did. She now talks about getting away from the systems and the laws that keeps us bound by speaking of one day owning her own business. In my take, I think that's great for a starting point. A starting point is the first step in overcoming the laws that bind us.

Without this, a plan to combat this system almost always ends with us losing in the long haul of our battle. Laws over the years have been created for you and me, and I thank God much for them. For example, the Equal Employment Opportunity Act of 1972 states that any race has an equal right to be employed, period. Or the Fair Housing Act of 1968 that states the policy of the United States to provide, within constitutional limitations, for fair housing throughout the United States.

These are just a couple of laws that built America's diversity for years before I was born and for years to come. These are the laws that we look for to produce assistance for us in our push for protection legally.

But what about the laws that are created for me and unto me but are not helpful to me, instead doing more harm than good by placing me in a bracket that doesn't help but instead hurts me?

For example, the Equal Pay Act of 1963. The basis of this law is that every one (up until 1997) will receive for their so-called hard work four dollars and twenty-five cents an hour.

In my biased opinion, this is one of those laws that seem to be lawful for me, but after further studies concerning myself, I feel that you will never get paid for what you are truly worth, so four dollars and twenty-five cents is a slap in the face.

Whatever a base pay is for an employee can't compare to the currency that generates from up top that we as employees never see while in the system. When these base pays are set for the employees, it's good to remember that the owner or the people that set the pay rate don't have our best interests in mind for us to succeed as people or employees. For a person to recognize this truth makes these so-called laws non-expedient to me. To grasp that, take it in, and accept that can be a very difficult pill to swallow.

I had to find out the hard way that when you understand that the system is built only to appease those that are the owners, your views on the system will change dramatically and the question isn't where can I find a better job, but the question is how can I get out of the job circuit once and for all.

Each and every day (until I reach the point where I want to be) I read and try to associate myself with only things and people that are expedient for me. That in itself is a change that all of us can stand to deal with. With the pending mindset that persuades us that the nine-to-five system is where it's at, we need a fast-growing dose of things and people that are expedient to us.

We need people that can and will have a major influence on what we are trying to accomplish in our life. We also need a method and a strategy that will overcome those pending laws that make the system what it is and has been for years.

I honestly believe that once this is created and mapped out, then and only then will we see the laws of the system buckle to our decision to overcome them and to not be brought under the power of any anymore.

Before I was terminated on October 3, 2007, there was what seems to me, laws that had suddenly been implemented in to our job description only to keep us under the power of the system. I will say now what I did then, the guy that prearranged these sudden laws was a jerk, a pain in the butt, and an all out loser.

A job was posted on the Internet for an executive security position at the site where I worked. (This knowledge came after someone else got the position instead of this fellow security guard.) It was told to us (employed security workers) that about a week or so after that job was posted here came Mr. Jerk. Already a couple of weeks into his brand new executive security employment, he immediately wanted to insert his laws that weren't for the company's best interest, but to keep all of the employees at bay with these bad laws, forcing us to make a choice to quit or stay and be bought with the power of these sudden laws. "From the information that I have gathered thus far, many of you have been with this company for a long time and that's great, but just like everything, at one point, life needs a change, and that's why I'm here to make sure that change happens." Mr. Jerk said.

"Some of you may like that change and some of you won't. Those of you who do will stay on the bus. Those of you who don't will be put off the bus."

"One thing that I will change around here is that people who are already here working on shift will stay and work if someone calls off, instead of supervisors calling someone from home to come in and work," he stated. That was one of his many laws that was implemented by him that I believe was bondage. Why would you want an employee, after already working an 8 hour shift, to work additional hours instead of calling someone in who may not have worked that day or have less that forty hours for that week? It is plain to say that power in and of the system always leans in the direction of the one who has all the control. It didn't matter at all to him that people had started that job without anything and slowly moved up in position and pay. All that he was concerned about was the fact that power played a big role in who he was and dominated the workers that were on the bottom of this company. Before I was terminated, at least seventy-five percent of the employees that were there before me either were fired or quit. He called it change. I call it control. I don't think any of us that worked for that company wanted an easy street. All we wanted was to do an efficient job, go home, and do it all again the next day. But Mr. Jerk didn't want that; he wanted power and not change.

The job duties were easier than tasting pie all day, but the laws that Mr. Jerk interwove weren't meant to be easy but to enchain us to the point that we really didn't have power in and of ourselves.

Change is one of the most important devices that any one person can have, but if change only comes to rob you of your decision-making ability, that's a big problem. A memory that I always keep in mind is the fact that the system is always one up on us. They have laws, power, ability, and most of all money. Out of those four, I believe that everyone has ability.

We all have the capacity to recognize when something is going wrong in and out of our lives—that's the ability. And when we come to grips with this ability, and the fact the at least 99.9 percent of jobs could care less about who you are, where you going, and why you want to go there, then we will be one up on them. It's a natural belief to feel free, comfortable, content, and excited about where we are in the system, but when the question keeps arising in our minds that second-guesses the operation of this system, then we know that we are on the right track to move out of that system.

I always have given the benefit of a doubt when I was on my up and down the road within the system. I never knew that I have ability to change where I'm going, not by laws that constrain me, but by a mind and people that are expedient to me. As I have been speaking about in one of my earlier chapters, the system should be used as a platform for us to move into a bracket of life where we can overcome and see better for ourselves. My life in the working field hasn't been that great, but there have been times that I recognize that great can come out of me by understanding that the system is a bridge between work and faith.

The more I think about that, the more I smile. I smile because I ride on the wave that no matter how much the systems all across the US try to cover up what they are really about, I will not allow my life or your life to be hampered by it as long as I have a voice.

There is no way that the systems of our world should be replicating what they have been doing since the foundation of the earth. Yes, there are laws that are lawful unto me, but the question lies: are they expedient to me?

Are they beneficial for my future, my children's future, or for those that I have relationship with on a daily basis? If the answer is no they are not, then there should be a strategic plan through prayer, faith and action on our part to get out as soon as possible before it is too late.

Our lives depend on substance that we all can prosper on and not laws that bring us under power to one that doesn't have our best interests in mind.

CHAPTER 6

Disconnect the Life Support System

"All paid jobs absorb and degrade the mind."
- Aristotle

As my mind journeys into the realms of my thoughts, and my eyes open to what I see, I smile with great joy before reality sets in and I'm brought back to earth, quickly moving from those realm of thoughts.

Many of us may not say what I just quoted, but many of us have similar thoughts that keep us headstrong into the mode of working and not into the realm of thoughts that will get us out of the system. I don't know about you, but I believe one of the best things going on in the world today is information that we can retrieve from the Internet.

One thing that has been so vital and of all importance to me is reading. So as I was surfing and reading, I came across something that struck me as reality. Our mind just doesn't think and operate from our central nervous system, but it is also a reaction mechanism. Our mind reacts to things in such a way that it affects our going and coming on a daily basis. And the quote above this chapter explains it.

Around March or April of 2001, I had just landed a job with the security company that I talked about in much of the early chapters, and at that time it was a great achievement for me. I had locked down a third shift position. My family consisted of me, my wife, her daughter, and my son. We would all be set for a pretty non-struggling lifestyle. All that had my mind coming and going in the area of money!

I spilled my energy and my desire to a corporation trying to put more money in my pocket, to establish a well-balanced family from a money perspective, only to be knocked backwards on my butt by the company gurus, who stated plainly that your long and hard hours are just not good enough.

Before the third shift position gave me a lock for a full time shift, I worked three shifts in one day just to get hired on there. Once again, this was by far the best thing that happened to me in the job industry. As time moved on, I saw that my family suffered, not from my desire not to work, but from my job not working.

It would take me a couple of years to figure out that my job was causing me so much stress and so much time—my family saw less and less of me. The mode of thinking in this scenario of life is that the best will come when you land the best paying job out there.

Your family is fine, you're making money, and there is a little more on the table to eat than there was last week. You want to find some common ground that would support your working day and night, time away from family, headaches from the job, and money, even though you hate being around your fellow employees. It all comes crashing on your shoulders like a ton of bricks.

It's bad enough when you find yourself losing what has been dear to you for the last four years, then to see your job, your money-maker, you bill-payer become your biggest burden in secret.

Although we skip the burden for more hours on the job, we can't help but notice the mindset that tells us at least every other day that this is too much on my body, I need to quit. Before we recognized what's going on, our mind has suffered a major lapse and we are pressed to find answers that will heal our hurting soul.

How can someone start a job, work to the best of their ability, get a paycheck every two weeks, but find himself taking on more than just the job duties that are required by the system?

For a long time in my life I couldn't figure this question out. Meetings were being held on a regular basis concerning this nine-dollar-an-hour job like we were major owners in a law firm and we were on the verge of getting more money.

We didn't discuss issues that would change who we are or discuss things that would make us better people in society, but we discussed how bad we were doing on this job. Still in the confines of my mind this job was so important to me, I paid the meeting no attention. I just focused on working more overtime.

As the system continued to work its master plan on the lives of the employees, we were slowly being drawn to a degrading state that left us questioning: aren't we better than this, can't we do better than this?

"Aren't we better than this?" That remains a question eight years later. For others it remains a question for a great deal of their life and then some. No matter how much I tried, I could never rid myself of that question. I only covered it and tried to sweep it under the rug.

None of us could get past it; we all felt the after effects of the absorbance that had taken place in those meetings. We all suffered; it wasn't a single person that worked for the company that was at the bottom of the totem poll that did anything to defend themselves that day. We all looked and acted as if there wasn't any hope for ourselves.

It was already bad enough that we were working our hearts out and not seeing the greatest of labors being manifested, but to degrade us openly seemed to be worst. Just like every negative report that we received on a job, we have a comment or comments that throw daggers at the report, convinced that this paid job is not worth the headaches that comes along with this.

But as the end result unfolds and we are finally faced with a decision, the thing that our minds absorb the most is that no matter how bad this job gets, we are going to continue to work it no matter what. I dreamed this, I rehearsed it, and I talked about it silently without anyone else. I was totally convinced that all of this was right, no matter what was going on at my job.

It didn't take long before I didn't have a family, and backpedaling to a whole different lifestyle was what I had to face. That wasn't a bad experience that I went through, just a new lesson learned that taught me that everything that my mind absorbed during those years concerning my job degraded me.

Yesterday I spoke with the same friend of mine who I speak with almost every day. Of course, just like many of us, she works a nine-to-five, literally. The conversation stemmed once again, like it always does, from not enough income and the disrespect that she received from some of her coworkers.

Just like I felt all of my job life then and up until now, the system is only built for two things: to generate money, and to bring people like you and me there to market their product at their rate, period. She went on to tell me that she always feels like she is on the rebound when it comes to her paycheck, moving up in the company, and working extra hours. The difference from me working a paid job and working for myself is simple: control over my own life and not having control over my life.

"Michael, I understand that, but I don't think that's where God has me at right now. I want to own things and pay cash for them but right now this is where I think God has me."

"Alright, but I do want to tell you that the nature of the system is the job force that each of us will face on a daily basis that keeps us connected and sometime that keeps us from hearing God's true word."

The conversation immediately switched to something else.

Before it did, I told her I respect her view but for me it's a much different outlook.

(If you are reading this now, I love you, friend.) The nature of a person or animal has a small to slim chance of changing when they both continue to do the same thing all the time and that's putting it mildly. The main reason is simple; what they have been doing for so long is enough for them no matter how bad it is.

Now, speaking about the system (job) that has a zero percent chance of changing to fit the needs of you and I. We work hard everyday. We spend more time in the system than we do in that house we went in debt to get while wondering why we feel so depressed from the absorption that we cling to every single day that we work.

Those of us that work and are employed by a major company overall are losing. We are losing with the fact that states that our ownership mentality (those of us that have it) is being dismissed the more we allow the system to tell us from working each day that this is where it's at. It would be a disheartening thing when I get fifty or sixty years old and my two sons ask me what did I do so great in life. And if my response is that a paying job was my life's highlight, then I could honestly say my life was in vain.

When I was a bit younger than I am now, I was captivated by a question that always puzzled me. I never asked anyone concerning my question, I just kept it to myself. One reason that I didn't ask anyone was the fact that I may be aggravating and getting on someone's nerves. Then too I didn't want to be looked at as dumb or perhaps joking somewhat with a question that I should already know the answer to. The question that got to me so was: what is it like to be on life support?

I know already what you're thinking: good you didn't ask anyone that question? The reason this question peaked my interest was the truth that a person can actually be dead but somehow be alive based on a hospital machine. After a long while, I didn't think much about it until more cases were on the radio, television, and in adult conversations that I heard from time to time.

As I got older and came into new information, I realized that the patients on this machine really weren't alive, but they were dead. When hooked up to this machine, it causes families to grieve more, worry more, and spend more money in doctor bills to keep that patient going, and more than anything it prolongs death. Some people feel very strongly against the use of life support and issue a do not resuscitate

(DNR) order.

After some point, between the life support system and that patient never coming around, the family decides that death is the best for the patient and pulling the plug on this life support system will be the best for all of us. I look at the whole entire life support technique and realize without a shadow of a doubt that as long as I have been in the paid job industry, I have been on life support.

Many may not agree with that or accept it for themselves, but I can; that's why I wrote this book.

There was not only pain inflicted on me, but also on my family. I couldn't live outside of myself. As long as I wanted to make a career out of the system thinking it will be the savior of my life, then life support became my life. It's hard to pull the cord when so many people care about you, love you, and cherish you to the utmost.

Many tell you, including your family, that the system in the long run will benefit you in your old age. But I found that to be as wrong as two left shoes. Just like the literal life support system, you depend on it for everything—including your life.

Your next breath, your thought process, and the way you act and feel all depend on the life supported by the system. It's funny; when you tell someone (just like I stated earlier) that you want to break free from the life support system. They either tell you not to do it until you find something better, or it's going to be too hard to break free.

Something better? Tell me, what's better? Going from one nine-to-five to another nine-to-five? Oh, I know—just change from first shift to third shift. That way we will get a quarter more raise on the hour. Here, do like I did and work a full-time third-shift security job from eleven PM to seven AM, then work a part-time first-shift airport job where you're unloading heavy freight, bringing that freight inside the warehouse, breaking it down, placing it in its respective place of destinations in a dock port, then finally going home at eleven AM if they decide that everything is to their satisfaction.

Sounds like fun, right? Or for me, an absorbance of all that work mentally then a degrading of the mind. That life support living at its finest that doesn't get you anywhere but just one more step to your working past the next day. How dare someone tell you that an advancement in life is just another nine-to-five with a extra quarter on the dollar?

Even the great Greek philosopher Aristotle realized that the nine-to-five syndrome is a system that hinges upon a life support mentality that makes you feel less than not who you can be, but who you are. His statement was blunt and to the point: *all paid jobs absorb and degrade the mind.* What did he mean by this powerful statement? It's simple; the nine-to-five system eventually kills who we are and replaces with a counterfeit you that works in the system usually forever, humiliating us mentally.

Aristotle was a man who never experienced the system nor knew what the life support was in a job setting. Not only was he a Greek philosopher but also a teacher of Alexander the great, one who wrote on subjects like physics, metaphysics, poetry, theater, logic, rhetoric, politics, government, ethics, biology and zoology. This man knew exactly who he was and used faith as his mechanism. Now to some of you that doesn't mean anything, but those of us that find the nine-to-five syndrome to be a dead-end road to failure that absorbs and degrades our mind keeping us from our destiny, thank you for giving me your ear.

But somewhere along that road, Aristotle discovered that his life was too important to waste it away by the voice of "just get a better job." For his efforts he goes down in history as one of life's great philosophers that has an active academic study in schools today since he didn't degrade his mind with a paid job. So tell me, how long will you be on life support before you say just as Aristotle did, *all paid jobs absorb and degrade the mind?*

CHAPTER 7

"Don't expect something great from something you didn't create..."

- Michael Arnold

I heard it out of the mouth of my coworker: "You know you did something great when you're not in a cubicle anymore." I looked across from me as the strong bold words procceded out of his mouth while we did security tours in the huge investment building. I didn't understand right away why he said that, but after his large smile and a man dressed extremely nice walked past us, I instantly became enlightened.

This young tall blonde hair guy talking on his cell phone with an extra-elegant suit walked as if he owned the place. If he didn't own the place, it was possible he was on his way to owning it or something in life by the way he carried himself.

When you wake up in the morning, I wonder what is it that you say out loud to yourself? Maybe your significant other hears it every day so they tend to ignore you. For me I said numerous things from "Man, I wish I can lay in the bed for a couple more hours" to "God, I hate this stupid job!" to "Man I wish I could find something else; I'm tired of working that job!" (That's probably my all-time favorite one.)

The great part about those morning and night quotes (depending on what shift I worked) was that all they ever amounted to was just words formed into sentences that no one really cared to hear. Fellow employees don't care to hear about the job being stupid, or that we're tired of being there. (Next time try asking them, and see if they will sit around the break room table and listen to you.)

All they care about is seeing the employer place a check in their hand (while angry because they have to stop what they are doing to give it to you if you don't have direct deposit). They go and cash it, pay bills, and whatever else is left do whatever with it. One thing that those morning, midday, and night speeches taught me was just because I was part of the job and getting a paycheck every other week and I was paying my bills, that wasn't a life that was anything close to resembling anything great.

Words uttered by my coworkers, friends that I speak with, and even family members stress the issue that a job with great pay and great benefits is a great place to work. Now the word that I hear a lot is "retirement." I'm thirty-three years old. Tell me a nine-to-five job I can retire from and benefit from for the rest of my life. I have no clue, so maybe you may know someone since you believe the same thing that I believe.

I have yet to find any nine-to-five that I can wake up and smile about, because I know without a shadow of a doubt that where I am off to is short-term and long-term will bring me something or somewhere great. I have yet to experience that. Have you?

I'm single at this time, but somehow I remain optimistic in this land of (some) women that seem to be overwhelming picky. Lately the marriage phenomenon has taken the world by storm, especially in the church community. Everyone feels that their life would be that of greatness if they get married.

The few women that I have spoken with in the last year strongly believe that a man that doesn't have himself together isn't worthy of their hand in marriage. Upon further conversation they give great details that a man that has himself together is one that has a car, his own place of residence , and most of all a job!

For the most part of their thought process, these women feel that a twenty-dollar-an-hour job or more is better than a man shaping and forming his destiny. I don't know about the men who are reading this right now, but for me this approach in a women choosing a man has had me dangling by the wayside.

I always thought, from a child growing up to now a full-grown young adult, my object of center was to have a good job and hopes of a good woman one day that will accept me because of my good job. In the end that whole blueprint was slowly coming undone and I was left with a blank piece of paper. Just like that day I mentally held that blank piece of paper up before me, I realized that the significant part of that piece of paper is that it was vacant and blank; containing nothing.

It now held the empty space that voided out the thoughts of those women that found that what men acquire from something that already exists is great without question. The backside that also had been blueprinted with the irresponsible thoughts of some men that make mention more times than one that if they want to get ahead, the best thing they can do is live footloose and fancy free with a woman and not pay anything. She pays his way. (I know some people like this.) But the sheet that hangs in the face of my mental eyes showed me that both of these incidents from women and men's expectations, in their eyes to be of something, can wind up being nothing.

It's strange that we desire something that we did not create but have great expectations concerning it, just like the systems we work in on a daily basis.

Why is that? If I have zero and I find a woman that I want or desire in marriage, why do I expect something out of that woman that I think will advance my life and I don't have power to advance myself? Some women in the world that I have met along this path of life expect a man to have a job only so all of their bills could be paid, and somewhere down the road they desire strongly to succeed on the expense of the man's job. Let it be known very quickly that I said that will not happen with me. That's a dream that turns into a nightmare in a matter of moments. I haven't forgotten about the friends that I used to have who spoke contently concerning their strong and admirable desire to freeload constantly on a woman's house, car, and money and they have nothing to deposit in the relationship . How sad and pathetic.

With those two examples I know you can think of people that may be friends of people who live like this, and then all of a sudden their expectations for something out of the situation never materialized. Why did this happen? Thank you, I'm glad you asked. Many of us will agree convincingly that in order to advance in life we have to be somewhat successful in our strategies . Many have found the key and unlocked the door and have stepped into their success with simply no effort. These people I called gifted or geniuses.

Others like myself had to work extremely hard, and then harder if that wasn't hard enough to get the job done, see success on a more lower level, but still succeed since it's our creation that invents who we are. Now, those of us can see that from many different ways, angles, and positions that may suit us. That's fine.

But when you look to invent yourself or think you are inventing yourself on the expense of someone else, it doesn't work versus creating out of yourself, and that is the reason why so many of us suffer in the long-run: because we want to be great by way of someone else.

This is something that is pumped and primed into our young people on a daily basis even when attempting to become an entrepreneur (which I will speak about later). Not to get ahead of myself here and talk prematurely about my other topics coming up, having the heart of an entrepreneur gets you in the executive chair and will carry you into greatness. But the nine-to-five job, which we chase after daily, will leave us only with a pension and an expectation no larger than just a better nine-to-five job for our kids.

When I was married (the best thing that happened to me in 1997), she and I talked confidently about success and how bad we wanted it in our life. I could never renounce my words that said I will be great when I get a better paying job! That was my mind, my soul, and my heart.

58

Nothing meant more to me at the time than a job paying wages of at least twelve dollars and up. This would be my moment of "greatness," if I could land this. She talked not about her getting a job (which was fine, I didn't care; she was my wife so she didn't have to work), but me getting that job of what would be greatness to me. Her main objective was hoping to see me land that job, so when I did, guess what, she did as well.

I applied for jobs that I knew I didn't qualify for like a plumber, CDL truck driver, and jobs of that sort. My mind was so consumed with achieving just money I had no earthly clue that all those jobs that I had applied for didn't have one thing to do with me being great.

Don't get me wrong, I thank God totally for all the jobs I had over the years, but in terms of them making me great, that would be like a mud bath making a pig clean. In learning that, it wasn't so hard to accept when I found that my heart was pulling away from the system. That was my thought and still is: that I could not be great from a job that I didn't want to be in or associate myself with forever.

In reinventing ourselves, we find out that it heals the wound that the nine-to-five job has inflicted on us over the course of the years. The more we relay to ourselves that it's OK to deal with this nine-to-five temporarily and move on from it later, the better we will feel and the more free we become.

If I was reading this book for the first time I would scratch my head, breathe, then tell myself how much of a challenge it would be to first break away totally from the nine-to-five mentally that may correspond with my heart, and then take steps to see something I never saw happen in my life. People come up with all sorts of gimmicks for their lives to become better, some of them good, but most of them not so good.

I have heard of people giving money in church, working more hours on their job, getting more than one job, working a better job, and saving money. I tell you, people have a ton of what they believe that will change a person from the nine-to-five blunder we suffer from for years to a person of greatness.

There are thousands of job in my city and millions all across America that have some sort of retirement, pay rate, 401K plans, and pension plans that lure us in, giving us the feeling that now we got it, now I'm going to make it, now I'm going to rise to the top, now my life will be good, I will finally make it now. A year later, two years later, five years later, however long the process, the ball fumbles in our hand, we drop it and there goes our whole idea to finally win one down the drain.

There wasn't a time when I got fired from a job, except my last termination, that I didn't blame the job in a way that they should have given me something. And even before I got terminated as well, I always wanted something from that job. A job that I worked for right before I got a divorce finally decided that they didn't want me anymore so they fired me. (I guess I got a two-birds-with-one-stone deal.)

I was totally beside myself. I just thought they were in error. Let me just make this note. Most of the time the nine-to-five is in error when they fire you; they just obtain so much more power than you and I until we make ourselves unable to contest it in most cases. I felt more optimistic about my last termination since I knew that unemployment benefits were out there, but quickly came to grips with reality once I realized that when it runs out you're back to square one. So we ask ourselves: what is the point?

The job fired me, laid me off; whichever one, I was still jobless. I didn't get employment by another job right away, so that set me back in my bills. I cried (not literally, but I wanted to), complaining about how bad the job screwed me up, how I didn't received my unemployment benefits, and how bad I hated everyone there. Yeah, it got that bad. I felt as though I could not go on. I wanted something from this job and what I wanted I thought it would bring me greatness.

In the earlier months of 2004, I developed a strange feeling, something that I call my "afflatus moment"(I will speak more in depth about this later). Out of nowhere it shot through me. It was my heart finally giving an impulse to my mind to believe what it was believing. It was like the two of them being in a fifteen-year board meeting concerning my life.

This imparting of knowledge and inspiration, or what I called my "afflatus moment," gave me a sudden reality check beyond my comprehension. My view concerning jobs and their outlook on employees brought a new chapter in my life. My level of expectation for the nine-to-five reached extreme heights, and more than at any point in my life I was ready to take off, but as my afflatus moment didn't outgrow my expectation for the nine-to-five, all of those thoughts of just a better job rescinded with the passing of the wind.

I learned that it was OK to get fired and to be without a job. The owners owned the company; they are the giant gurus that make their company what it is on a creative echelon. As the experience went on, it also relayed to me the message that what I haven't created or formed from nothing into greatness I shouldn't expect to get something great out of it. The form, the blueprint of success, falls on those who have the vision to create.

That meeting of my mind and heart that meet several years ago is now slowly registering into a way of life that tells me I'm not of the system but a man of greatness, and no longer will I fret and complain about a system that I didn't create but feel I should get something great out of it. Many of you may not see the light of day and the nine-to-five syndrome seems stronger than ever in your life, absorbing and degrading your mind with low pay and extra hard work, but understand that the meeting between your heart and mind is just a little longer than you expected. In due time, you will know that whatever you chose to create will be many times more effective than that nine-to-five burden that tells you that you can't get it because you didn't create it. Just say to yourself secretly, "My afflatus moment has arrived and I will win!"

CHAPTER 8

Is it Legacy or are you just Passing Through?

That moment was definitely a turning point in my life and an eye-opener that defined who I am and who I would become in the future. The job industry was still a thorn in my flesh seeing that the break I needed to break free physically wasn't there yet. In the fact that your break isn't upon you to reinvent yourself, you still have all the right to think creatively before the manifestation comes upon you even in the midst of the system.

I will repeat it again: if the nine-to-five is your place of stance right now that's fine, as long as you know it is your bridge that will lead you into a form of creativity and ultimately make you great; by all means, use it for the time being. The system has always been employed by people and groups of people who look to the best interest of themselves, not just with the gaining of wealth, currency and the adding of more muti-million dollar companies. They are also after the stripping of the employees' desires to do better with low pay per hour, bad medical insurance, or in some case no insurance at all. They give us false hope into believing that the nine-to-five is advancement, a place to retire from. The system gives us a break throughout the eight-hour work day but refuses to give us ways to improve, just like they did when they started their business.

But what we learned last chapter is that it's all right. Since we didn't create it, we don't expect to become great from it. The afflatus moment not only inspired me to break free from the system, but it also showed me that repeating it in any shape, form, or fashion long-term will only bring me back to where I once started, and that is right in the arms of disappointment.

My life thus far has been equipped with many restrictions and shapeless acts that I thought were making a difference in my life, but the only thing that it was doing was turning me around, facing me in the same direction, and repeating myself all over again. Someone may say just do something differently and you won't have to go through that again. Good theory, but not that easy.

All the points that I have made in my earlier chapters were great points and for me life-changing. But even with life-changing points, the question still lies: why is the system employing more people a day than entrepreneurs a year?

For me and my thought process, that's stunning. The reason why it's stunning to me is that the mind has so much power over us; we will do something continuously knowing that it will hurt us instead of helping us. One thing I could remember doing as an adult, more than a few times is engaging in the strip club life and spending hundreds of dollars per week when I knew that the money should have gone to a more profitable cause.

Let me just say this, if any of you engage in that lifestyle that's all right for you, I have nothing against that, but for me it was just bad news! I could not recover from the one to two nights over a period of time turning into four nights a week. It was total madness spending money like I was drinking water effortlessly.

I knew this late-night activity wasn't for me, but I engaged in it over and over and over again. This was the type of activity that resonated in my brain like the thought of a brand new marriage in the clef of a private island amongst people of the same caliber. More than just the act, it was the expression of the act, the residue, the thing that lingers after the act.

My heart's strong desire during that time, to continue on in that lifestyle, was more felt than where I needed to be going.

So the most part of those crucial years I was pondering in the sand, trying hard to overcome this battle between the strip club and I. Finally, after a total of five years (2001-2006), I discovered that I lost the fight and the afflatus moment was all over me, so I gave in to that instead of another year of the strip club lifestyle.

I was lucky to get out of that circumstance with my mind still intact. To be honest, I thought the world of that lifestyle and wonder today if I could do it all again, would I change anything? Tough question, but I have an answer, and that answer is yes I would change something.

What I would change wouldn't be the desire to go to the strip club, but the desire to change my outlook on the strip club. My belief system was to go have a good time, spend money, and go home. If that strip club could speak and tell how it felt, it would say, "Michael Arnold, I thank you kindly for your time and most of all your money. You're just like the majority of the people who come here, you're just passing through. Goodbye and good night, Michael."

Now, I don't know about you, but I would feel rather offended if a person told me that. But the club—I don't think I would ever return again after it spoke those words to me.

Just think about that for a moment in reference to the system, your place of work, those long, hard hours of going above and beyond for the employer—or should I say the owner, since it is his company.

Everyday, or on a regular basis, he comes directly to you and bluntly relays the messages that the work you do is only to profit him because you are just an employee and you don't have any part of anything here but the tools you have to do my job.

Well, guess what? The more we find ourselves in a working space between two doors, the front and the back, they don't have to tell us because we tell ourselves each and every day that we are theirs; we belong to them until those eight hours are up.

Not by any means do I claim to be Aristotle, William Shakespeare, or any of the literary geniuses who had a keen understanding concerning their genres, but it doesn't take a rocket scientist to figure out the term "passing through" may have a change in a person's decision-making. My basic definition (briefly) that defines passing through is: coming and going without anyone knowing you were ever there. (Doing the same thing without making any impact on anyone or anything.)

The next statement might not be received by everyone, but it is expedient to all who read this. A great example of "passing through" simply is a person going in debt to purchase something, never changing you or you're surroundings, working in the system for years, never finding that bridge that takes you from the nine-to-five to greatness. (Don't worry; I have been there more times than one.) You are "passing through," never changing anything, just coming then going.

It makes me sick to my stomach when I hear a woman say she won't date a guy without his own place, car, and a job, even if it just happened to that man and he is in rebound mode. What about you women? Are you really that great and better than him, or are you just like most, just "passing through?" That's a question we all need to ask ourselves, and then we won't be quick to jump to conclusions concerning where that person stands in life. For the record, if or when you meet someone (if you already have someone, congratulations, tell me your secret) the question may come up, "what are you bringing to the table or what do you have?"

That's a good question, but if they start talking confidently about their house, their car, and other material resources that they depend on like a broken-down crutch, and God knows if they mention their nine-to-five bondage hole, GET AWAY FAST!

All right, thanks a lot for bearing with me on my notable reference.

"Passing through" is not just a quote, but it is definitely a way of life for many people in America. Seriously, we all have come to a place somewhere in life where we adapted more to the nine-to-five than anything else, and so that makes us more apt to find anything that's different and uncommon to us far out and ridiculous.

Conversations continue to be part of what seems to be a habit to me. I speak with people daily concerning my life and their lives and other issues that spark our interest. With that said, the same young lady that I spoke about earlier—we talked again recently about the same thing, her job.

"I don't know what I'm here for, Michael; I'm not happy, I don't have any joy in my life, and I hate going to that job," she said. My word and thought acted simultaneously with control instead of an outburst.

"You know Michael; I had it all before I moved here to Charlotte. I don't want you to think that I was rich or anything like that, but I had everything. I had a nice house, a car, and I could go out to eat wherever I wanted. Since I moved here it's been the opposite. I don't know what to do. I've been praying for I don't know how long about this." My thoughts were doing well, but my mouth wanted to open before my thoughts closed its thinking process. After everything had seemed as if it stopped and my thoughts were finishing thinking, then I had the liberty to speak. I was glad that my thought had a better hold on my mouth than I did so I wouldn't say the wrong thing to her.

"You know that you're a single woman, right?"

She paused a brief moment, then spoke what would have come to any that were asked that question. "Yeah, why do you ask that?"

"The reason I ask that is because I wanted to tell you that you can do more for yourself and people can pattern their life after you with the liberty you have to what you want to do." "Don't worry about not having what we all have, be concerned about the legacy that few people have."

She listened attentively. "I just don't want to pass through; I have two sons that I have to account for, and it won't be just working the nine-to-five. I want to establish a legacy for them. I don't care about houses, car or any of that stuff we all can get that."

"What about the establishment for one life?"

She didn't say anything so I knew I still had her attention. "God has given me something greater than the nine-to-five, and that greater is the desire to write, and that writing will become my legacy." I felt good about saying that even though she wasn't enthused about it. Our conversation ended from that point and I hung the phone up.

Many have told me (and still tell me), "You can't be a writer, and it's too hard. Don't quit your job until you know you have a sale. It's dumb to just focus on writing and forget your job and not have an income."

To everyone reading this book, in case you didn't know, this is my third book. When I started writing this one, I had been jobless for the last three months. They wanted to take my car because I was one month behind. No money. If I wanted to buy a ninety-nine-cent hamburger I couldn't do it, but I want to explain this to all of you. Every time that I get in front of my computer and start to write and work on my projects, it's a peace, a joy. No pressure, no system to deal with, no one calling expecting me to be working at a place that I didn't create but expect something great out of, my mind is not absorbed and degraded by a paid job that's killing me everyday!

Every day that I think about my mom and two sons, I understand this is for them. Every time that I think of just a few people that will read this, I understand this is for them as well. So I will be broke if it will form my legacy, I will accept not being able to by a burger if one day I will be able to pay cash for my mom to be in a home, I will denounce the job circuit always if my destiny will be writing instead of security.

I don't want to pass through this life. I want a legacy.

Why? Because when my sons get my age they will never know what it's like to work their butts off in the nine-to-five system that kills dreams and promotes the owners' wealth. I won't allow it; not for my sons.

And to the people that read this, if the words of this book changes you mind and slowly breaks away from the system, I know then a legacy has begun in your life. Just like the people that question me, wondering why I write, wondering why you do and feel the way you do about forwarding your life and reinventing that dream. They can't relate because they're just passing through and your life is being written again with the legacy that you decide to leave for your children, your cousins, and those who will come after you. That dream that is covered up by that system, that nine-to-five syndrome that has most people locked, is now overriding with legacy, that thing that will not just inspire you to denounce the system but others as well. Many that feel that just passing through is OK; expect those people not to be in favor of you, laugh at you, call you dumb, and even to go as far as to tell you it's not going to work.

They told Fred Smith, creator of Federal Express, it wouldn't work; Walt's "dumb idea" created the Disney Empire; Sam Walton's Wal-Mart supersedes the nine-to-five system that many people thought he should have stuck to. The significance about these three people is that they just didn't pass through; they believed that the nine-to-five was a joke. The desire for them to become great spoke volumes of their words and statement through their legacy that will go for many years to come. The fact that many of us work everyday and never realize that the constant strain of going and coming on a regular basis puts us in a mode of questioning when is this going to end, this going to work everyday and not getting anything but a paycheck that's never enough.

For some that means nothing since that paycheck is just enough for you; you have your car, your, house, and what you think is the best of the three, your job.

But just like the eight-one thousand dollar homes that were lost to foreclosure in two-thousand and eight they thought the same thing. Something happened; it wasn't that they didn't want to pay the mortgage. The fact is that they couldn't pay the mortgage and the end result was foreclosure. Why? The passing through of working and not having enough money brought them to this point.

I know you feel just as I do sick and tired of the job industry. Each and every day that we work we become another victim of just passing through and not getting anything in the process. There is a solution to this madness; it is your dreams, your talents, and the mind to believe that those three things will get you out and where you need to provide for you and others.

There are people that will come after us and we don't want them to take on our debt, and our job that we just passed through and now that's what they are going to do.

Those people are better than that. Let's leave them with a legacy and not a mind to just pass through.

Part 2

Chapter 9

Invest in you, not the system

OK, ladies and gentleman. We are finally to the half-way point, and I say you all have been great, I must say with all honesty. I'm glad for all of you; thank you for spending your time with me here. It's been a rollercoaster so far, but with hope, we will straighten up and hopefully do away with all the exhilaration that has us in rollercoaster mode.

My heart is keen on finding the right way in life that would bring people in the know on where they're going in life when it comes to destiny. The number one reason why I am so heartfelt about it is simply because of the strains I had to face and the build-up that I felt time and time again that I would never make it.

I never knew at a young age that we could become something great no matter what. The job industry (the system) is comprised of a corporation that is hinged upon big money. That's fantastic for them, not for us. They have a so-called plan that seems to reach out to just about every working-class citizen out there. One of these plans that I am speaking about is called retirement. I have thought on this plan for a time or two, and I am now starting to ask the question, "Do they really believe that it works for their employees or is it just a way to keep employees happy?"

That was my question then and that's my question now. Let's go a little deeper, can we? When I look at the eternals of the employment plan called retirement, it is the point where a person stops employment completely and begins a monthly payday on the expense of the company that they have been employed by.

It is an investment institute. Sounds good, right? When I first heard of this plan I thought, *wow, you work on a job for a certain time and after you "retire" the company pays you? How much better can it get?*

But if it is so great then it should have a great retirement age, right? Well, I'll let you decide. One report says that the retirement age varies from country to country but it is generally between fifty-five and seventy. Another report conveys that the retirement age is mostly viewed as sixty-five.

In 2007, the retirement age for teachers in <u>France</u> is thirty-eight years after employment and age fifty for train engineers on the national railway. The retirement age in India for employees was raised from fifty-eight to sixty years in July 2007. In Malaysia, the retirement age has just recently been raised from fifty-five years to fifty-six years old. How does the system go about acquiring your retirement rate? In proportion to the years of work and the average wages, this is usually provided by the employer; this is how they get a monthly income concerning our retirement.

Another case is a Monte Carlo retirement plan allows users to enter savings, income, and expense information and run simulations of retirement scenarios. The simulation will show the probability that the retirement plan will work. That's what the Monte Carlo retirement plan says to us.

Let's look at another plan of retirement that goes hand-in-hand with what I'm talking about that has been around since the 1930s; this retirement plan is called social security. The act of social security is a little different from the retirement benefits in that the social security benefits is a percent of money taken out of your check every week or every two weeks as a way of you receiving a paycheck from the government at a certain age after you work.

For a lack of time, I won't go into all the information concerning social security, I won't bore you with that, but I will talk about some of the points that highlight the subject of this book and chapter that's so important to all of us when talking about social security. The fast fact concerning social security is that it was created in 1935 to protect millions of workers from poverty in their senior years (at least sixty-five and up).

To me this sounded like a perfect way, almost a flawless plan to save us in our retirement years, but just as we learned thus far, the system has a major flaw in this so-called system of poverty-free senior citizens.

In 1937 the required 2 percent parole tax to support this trillion-dollar system had gone up to 6.2 percent. Someone may say that's not bad. It has only gone up about 4 percent in seventy-one years. But what about the money that's in the social security pot today? Of course we know that a company that makes money spends money. So over the course of these seventy-one years, can you imagine how much money was spent out of the social security pot on other things outside of social security benefits for elderly people?

If I have a income of thirty-thousand dollars a month and that increases month after month but my primary bills are not taken care of, partly because I'm taking a portion of that thirty-thousand dollar monthly income and spending it somewhere else, well guess what: I go bankrupt.

The amount promised in benefits is far more than the system can afford to pay. For years, social security has taken in more money than it has paid out; but instead of saving these surpluses, the government spends them in other areas, placing a burden on the social security pot to obtain money from other areas for qualified elderly people.

Would you agree that if I had at least a fifty percent belief system that social security is the answer to all my hopes and dreams to a better prosperity lifestyle, I would be dreaming or perhaps having a nightmare? (Dreaming is a little too kind to associate it with this topic of social security being a life of prosperity.)

Whichever one that we go with, dream or nightmare, it is safe to come to the conclusion that social security will not work as a place of great retirement from those of us that are from the ages of eighteen to forty years of age. Has anyone ever benefited from it? The answer to that question is yes.

Not only has social security been a factor in getting the elderly money in the past to keep them where they need to be financially, it also has been great with issuing out disability checks and other special checks that are not associated with retirement.

According to the Social Security Reform, it is weak when it comes to providing long-term retirement plans in the future. In 1950, there were sixteen workers to support every one beneficiary of social security.

Today, there are just 3.3 workers supporting every social security beneficiary. Another source tells us that a thirty-year old worker (the system) will face a 27 percent benefit cut when he or she reaches normal retirement age. These are stunning accounts that have affected us as workers in America. For the minds of us that desire to journey away from truth, finding rest in complacency, we will not take heed to the retirement plan that doesn't free us but keeps us in bondage forever.

The system and all of its so-called resplendent ideas of a reform that aim at our retirement only put a stranglehold on our children that in return repeats the cycle. I can't imagine (and this is strictly for me) a life where I am depending on a structure that has not invested anything in me. Let me explain that.

Those of us that believe that the system is flat-out horrible at producing empowerment to its workers will also believe that an investment in one's self would be appropriate for the long haul of one's self. With Social Security, it is only enough to get you by and you only will receive it at a certain age. What do you do if you are a young person like me? Let's be serious, the chances of you and I receiving Social Security is like saying Michael Jordan never was able to play basketball.

I learned growing up primarily in the small town in North Carolina called Gastonia, how important I was to the neighborhood friends I grew up with.

It wasn't a time where we were happy to be separated from each other, not because we wanted to continue to play with our toys and run aimlessly around the community, but because we invested so much in each other. Don't get me wrong, our toys and our aimless wandering meant a great deal to us, but it was what we got out of each other that really meant something to us.

If all I had to look forward to was just the opportunity to play with our wrestling men and action figures, on a old cemented porch in the cold of a winter day after school or on a long, hot summer evening in the core of summer break, I would have failed to know who my friends were and put trust into something that we would soon out grow. That's similar to how the system works. I got to know my friends, not for what they had but for who they were.

I knew without a shadow of a doubt that knowing them would be meaningful to me in the long haul of things. We all (at the time) gave each other something that we expected since we invested in each other, and that was a close-knit friendship.

We believe wholeheartedly that since we work for a company year after year after year (or at least desire to work for a company for the majority of our life) then we automatically fall in the bracket of proper investment.

To be honest it is an investment, not as we think, but what is more true is that we invest in something called time. Can I say that again? We invest not in ourselves, but in time? What's so bad about that? You have to work somewhere, right? Well, that may be true somewhat, we have to have some sort of income in life in order to make our life move forward. What would have happened if I spent all of my childhood and adulthood hanging around people that did nothing but bad things? The more we hung out together, the more I felt like I wanted to do the same things that they were doing.

Before someone questions the integrity of my statement, I am fully aware of the proverb says, "I don't have to do the same thing my friends do just because they are doing it." Either they will draw you or you will draw them. So it's not a matter of not doing, it's a matter of who will draw who to do what. In the world of the system, we have learned thus far that they have come up with an arrangement that is similar to my friendship diagram that states that social security and retirement are the foundation of drawing us in.

There isn't a way that we can persuade them (social security and retirement) that our plan (whatever that is) is so much better; instead we live from paycheck to paycheck believing that at the end it would bring us into prosperous living by way of their retirement plan. I bought into it before but I refuse to buy into it again.

There's no way in hell that I will believe that a social security plan that is ripped with over-spending, and a retirement check from the job that I work at for thirty years, have truly invested in my well-being.

I don't know about you, but I just can't get with that theory. It's more than bad to already have a difficult life and then have to put up with a so-called plan of greatness that will seal my life financially at an old age.

The thing that I admire so much about early friendship as a child up until adulthood is that we cared so much about each other. We expected what was given to each one of us day by day.

Our friendship grew stronger because we invested in each other on a daily basis. Not only did we grow as friends, but we grew into partners. We became a partnership from the beginning of our friendship to the end. After I moved away years later, I realized how much we did things together and not as separate entities.

One thing that I will say prudently is that an investment is a partnership, not a withdrawal technique. If the system cared so much about us as we suspect, why isn't anything being done to help us financially before we get to be sixty or seventy years old? What methods of investment do we take before our elderly years?

There is a simple approach to beating these so-called retirement plans that at the end won't be there for us and it's called investing in ourselves. How do we do that? It's kind of like reversing the process.

Instead of thinking work, work, for the system for years and just receiving a measly paycheck (most of us), think what can I create that will give me a return not from what the system gives me, but what comes out of me that people can invest in and I make money from it. When we invest in ourselves, the system doesn't stand a chance in keeping us locked into a belief system that states that retirement is the answer. Let me just say this. Many people have told me time and time again that writing is not going to work and a nine-to-five job is the only way for me to have something.

I learned that those people would rather invest in something that gives them enough just to get by and they are not willing to take a chance on themselves. Many have said I will eat those words of not working the nine-to-five system again. I could care less. Investing in ourselves can at times be low, but at the end we will see that we will hold our head up high and say to ourselves, we made it and the rest is history.

We cannot continue to overlook our well-being, and continue each day that we go to work, to be controlled then overlooked, to compel into who we really are by a system that invests in itself and not in us. We are so much better than that. A true investor puts time in themselves not just to make money but to establish a way that money makes them money. Every job that I worked on in my life I believe is a multimillion dollar company. It just didn't get there from nothing. It got there by someone or a group of people investing in themselves and not in a job. It might have been a job establishing the foundation for the investment but after it is built, I bet for them it was well worth it.

One way I suggest to start is to start small with whatever it is you see yourself doing, and then continue to work it and watch it grow.

Chapter 10

Reality Check

"Your worth consists in what you are and not in what you have."

- Thomas A. Edison

Right now at this particular moment, this is my favorite chapter. Why? I'm glad that you asked, so now I will tell you with open arms. (Laughing out loud.) Two words: "reality check!" The definition of this statement: Let's ensure that we know the truth about something. (That's my definition of that statement; yours may be a little different.) Many of us feel like what we have is it, nothing else after that.

This isn't my favorite chapter thus far because I have the information to write on the statement "reality check" while throwing stones at someone and not looking at myself. No, that's far from the truth. I learned a long time ago that when I am trying my best to establish reasoning between myself and another person, I first have to know that the information that I give I can relate in some sort of way.

Toward the end of the last chapter, I made mention of people that I have come in contact with that told me verbatim that the nine-to-five is the only way I can go to have something good in my life. Reality check:

everyone will not be in agreement with *your* investment methodology. I had to learn that, like when my mother told me at sixteen years old that if I think that I am running the house where she pays bills then it's time for me to get out of her house and get my own. I hated those words; it was so hard for me to accept her words, because I was so overbearing when it came to growing up and abiding by her rules. She didn't have a problem whatsoever in straightening me out with a reality check. Let's ensure that we know the truth about something. After a while (a long while) I knew without a shadow of a doubt who was running the show.

The thing about a reality check that makes it so workable in our lives is that it never will lie to us. For example, if I became supervisor over a company (God forbid), a reality check for me would be, "Michael Arnold, this is undoubtedly a good position, but you will only get so far based on what you know concerning the system. Either you can use this job and the position as a bridge to your destiny, or you can invest your life and time into this system and if you're fortunate you will come out with a small social security and retirement check."

That would be my realty check; yours may be different under a different circumstance, but I hope under this one it would be similar. I managed to work the words and statements of other people's negative belief about my investment into my destiny. I analyzed their words and statements furtively, trying earnestly to come to a conclusion of why they believe in such a way. (No, I don't waste my time over hot chocolate and cupcakes worrying myself about it.) I realize that we think in terms of the right now instead of the tomorrow, and so it is a natural thing to believe or live by saying to a person that your nine-to-five is the most important tool a man has to his or her survival.

So instead of me getting upset, yelling at that person, telling them how wrong they are, arguing with them, I say "OK" to myself, move right along mentally so that I can walk into the next phase of where I need to go.

Many use the nine-to-five as a crutch their whole lives, never walking freely in what will give them freedom, not when they get home from work, but as they kick that nine-to-five goodbye. Instead of catching on to something that will invest in us, we go with the normal for the last however many years, ignoring the reality check. That reality check says to us without a stutter, "You are worth more than this." It tells a great deal of us that. Now I understand that everyone in the world will not want to be free from the nine-to-five system, but there are some people that do, so those are the people that I'm talking to.

For whatever reason some may not want to break free, others may not feel that he or she has time (in all actuality they don't have time, which I will go into in an upcoming chapter), and others are just flat-out consumed with the place that they are in, which is going to work every day looking forward to the bits and pieces that are given to them.

My writing means so much to me, just as your passionate desires mean the world to you. I had a conversation with my youngest son's mother recently and we talked about work. She had a desire to comment on how important and vital it is for a person to work. She went on to converse turning her direction toward her value, her significance, because she worked the nine-to-five. My input was little and brief.

I lost interest totally when she shot down my efforts of wanting to write books for a living and denouncing the system once and for all. What she said that stood out more than any part of the conversation wasn't that she shot my desire to write books for a living, but her self worth because of the system.

It's amazing how we believe that a company that tells us each and every day that we go to these different jobs that they don't care about us; we still embrace it like a newfound love. I didn't have to say much to dispute my dislike for the system; she walked out of her apartment that morning saying at least three times, "I wish I didn't have to go to work this morning."

When your self worth is hinged upon a job, how much is your self worth really? There are many comparisons in the workforce that keep us chasing more and more dollar bills. One comparison that we make is what we have accumulated over the months and perhaps years. What we accumulate is seen as an accomplishment worthy of placing in a category of great achievements.

You ask these people what is it that a person must have to be considered to be doing great. Those people will tell you like I been saying for the last several chapters now, house, car, clothes, shoes, jewelry, and a good paying job.

Like Aristotle, Thomas Edison's greatness came from what he created; their individual works spoke so loudly that they changed where they were presently at a place and stamped on all of us that read about them today. Thomas Edison didn't just discover the light bulb, but he also maintained his status as a businessman.

Aristotle, on the other hand, dominated his era in the art of writing. This Greek philosopher set different categories in his art by writing on several subject matters like zoology, poetry, theater, and logic. These two men built upon who they were and not what they had. (They invested in themselves—remember that?)

I'm sure they had a great deal to boast about, but there was too much at stake, too much to lose by focusing on what they had. In my opinion, I don't believe these men knew that they would be a mark that personified greatness when they started. They just did it because that's all they knew.

I believe that it is so easy for us not only adapt to the things we have only, but build around them as well. When a young man in high school wants to date a young women and he goes to her house for an interview session, the father of that young women always stress what the young man's parents have. (I know the interview session doesn't live in this microwave age today, but growing up as a kid it did.) It doesn't necessarily have to be school kids; it could also be young adults that get tangled in this web as well.

We are consumers in the fact that as a mother, we pray that our daughters grow up to marry a man that has a good job and can take care of them the rest of their lives. As fathers, we hope that our sons make the decision to get the best job in the city or out of town so when that woman comes, the son can place the fact that he has a good-paying job, and her hope of having lot of money will be fulfilled through and by the system.

Along the way with these dreams in hand, somewhere on this road a major reality check comes bouncing our way out of nowhere. Not only does that daughter get disappointed and the son find his days of struggling to make his wife happy, but they both find that what they have is more important than who they are.

Why did <u>Thomas Edison</u> so bluntly make the statement that I have written at the beginning of this chapter? It's simple. He thrived on believing that his worth superceded anything that he had, and by far that is what classified him as being important to all of us that exist in the world today when we hit a light switch.

Growing up my self-esteem level was lower than an ant on ground altitude searching for food to feed herself and her colony. I didn't feel like I fit with any popular group in the school setting, so therefore I looked at myself as low and my peers higher.

Soon after that the questions came, one by one, like: "How can I fit in? How can I be like them? Why wasn't I born to have that like them?" Those were just a few of my questions that had me in limbo for so long until I understood that what they had wasn't as important as I made it out to be.

Thomas Edison didn't grow weary in his strong confession that his worth was only associated with who he declared himself to be. He realized that whatever he had consumed had been overshadowed by his will to be a marketer. Many of us have no idea what that means or symbolizes. I saw many of those same classmates years later (after I graduated) fall victim to drug and alcohol abuse, crimes of all sort, and more than anything working in and for a system that has written a statement declaring that social security, retirement, and 401K is the answer for solving our money problems in our elderly years. Thomas Edison wasn't buying the idea that the system is worth more than his desire to market his greatness.

No one could tell him that the job industry would reimburse him for his hard work over the years with a paycheck and a retirement plan that we know now doesn't work. He was worth more than that and it showed mightily in his work. Not only was he an inventor, but he also held the title of a <u>businessman</u> which declared him as one of the ones in history that relied on himself and not on the system. Many of us will say time and time again that we hate our job and that we wish we could stay at home. Others will say, "I don't like my job, but it's paying my mortgage, and the car that in my driveway would still be at the car lot if it wasn't for my job."

It sounds good, it makes us feel like we are worth something to have a fifty-thousand-dollar car in the driveway of a hundred-and-fifty-thousand-dollar home that after it all is said and done, we pay double for both the car and the house. The thing that strikes me most about Thomas Edison and others that created greatness out of themselves is the fact that we don't know at all what they had; all we are aware of is them and what was so significant about them. People hinge their lives on what they have, but does what we have hinge on us? The answer is no! Here is a question that I would like to ask those of us that rely heavily on the belief that what we have is our self-worth. What happens if whatever it is that we thought that we had that defines us to be worth something is all of a sudden lost; could we get it back?

For an example, the money that you have in your bank account, that two-hundred-thousand-dollar house, all the clothes that you used your credit card to get, numerous cars in the driveway of that home, and your job that may pay you what you believe to be good money. I want to interject here for just a moment before I close out this chapter to tell a brief story that relates to this book and chapter.

I met this young lady in the latter part of 1997 and I believed that I wanted to date her and possibly marry her as well. Confidence was hard to come by seeing that she had a nice car, a house, and a job. Me, I didn't possess any of that; I was staying in an apartment with my sister. As time moved on, through conversation, we fell for each other. She didn't care

84

that I didn't possess any of those things, all she was concerned about was Michael Arnold. More time went on and we were soon married. Within two months of my knowing her we were an item, not because of what I had (I didn't have anything to offer but myself), but because of who I am.

Many people will try extremely hard to try and persuade you that your only hope is based on the job you have, and so we accumulate all of what others think is self-worth. I made up for lost time in finding a job, saving a little money from time to time, getting a license and a car, and being a husband.

Thomas Edison was so focused on destiny that the system was portrayed (by him) as being that of no worth. Why would I say that? I'm glad you asked, so therefore I will explain. I don't know if Thomas Edison ever worked a job or not, but he knew without a shadow of a doubt that whenever he made this statement, he was more passionate about him than a job that he had or didn't have. Who was Thomas Edison? He was a man that was totally posed with that of a marketer of his destiny instead of a consumer by what he had.

I believe that when we come into the knowledge that what we have has little or nothing to do with who we are from a sense of being someone of significant, then we will quietly change our view about thing and the way our life is going for us, and the gift to create something out of ourselves will start to grow on us.

CHAPTER 11

Moving from the Cubicle
To the Executive Chair

I think the problem with some of us is the fact that a change is almost an impossible task for us to perform, mainly because we are more focused on the instant things that keep us afloat even though they're not the best for us. With my life I can relate to this fact more than anyone with the job I have worked on for the last seven years before finally being terminated.

My belief is that we feel that if something is going well for us, no matter if it's somewhat of a strain, without hesitation, we will ignore our "afflatus moment" to be satisfied, content, and most of all comfortable so that the "afflatus moment" would pass by, and we can continue maintaining our self-desires.

So as the "afflatus moment" moves out like the sun behind the clouds in the concluding part of the evening, so are we still at the same place we were years ago. The question may come up, "Why change, why do something different if the start of what I'm doing is suitable to me?"

Those are more questions I had years ago and even recently, working on the same job for almost seven years, when I was asked why I don't leave and try for something better.

The answer that I had for them was, "Jobs are too hard to find, but if

I find something along the way, I will take it and quit my security job." In other words, what I was saying was I wasn't willing to move unless something tapped me on the shoulder and whisper to me, "Time to go, Michael!"

Other than that, I wasn't that adamant about leaving; although my job was taking a major toll on me, I just really didn't want to change jobs since I didn't know what another job would be like. We believe so fervently that longevity is perfect when you have extended your time greatly within the system.

The system is a genius at keeping us surrounded with incentives that will keep us there, like overtime hours, pay raises, double-time for holiday work, and a temporary position in the company. (My company didn't make us any promises to keep us there, but there are some corporate jobs that feel the need to do this.) With their promises, we go out on a rampage telling all of our friends about the positive incentive that we receive or we are all going to receive with a smile pasted on our faces.

Now, these jobs know if they cannot just get their hooks in us but keep them there, we won't find any reason to move out from where we are and view life from a different perspective. I have never in my life heard so many people talk about the great money that they are paid for working for the company, but fail to tell or speak about the position that wears them out each day.

If the job position seems to hold so much of a great payday, why can't that payday change our perspective of where we are and where we're going? The reason that I stress so firmly how important it is on where we are going is that where we are at this moment isn't so great if it's not beneficial in the long run.

Where we are today is a product of a plan, or for most just a flat-out decision to do the same thing yesterday and today; it is a result of that decision. From my thinking, it is so unbearable to be placed in a position by people we called employers, who use their power to hire people so that the system will stay powerful amongst their competition and we as the employee stay in a position, and because that position pays so much money to us nothing else is important. Not even that voice that tells us there is something better than this.

The most important thing you as an individual needs to know about the system is that the position will always be there. I said earlier that we are expendable. Let me elaborate on this a little bit concerning this chapter. With some of the bigger companies around the world that pay a little more money then the jobs that don't take much to get, you may be somewhat of a value to your company until either they downsize, you do something against company policy, or the company decides that it wants to go overseas.

So the question arises: "How valuable are we really if we can be taken out with those three actions within the job system?" When I think long and hard about that, it makes me more and more determined to make myself valuable for me and not for the big heads in the system. As long as a fact lives that hasn't been changed by legitimate evidence, than the fact will remain.

That means a whole lot to me simply because no matter where I work, I can be replaced. I don't believe that too many of us take that into consideration at the time until it's too late. One thing that I must say about working security for so long is that it makes you observant. (Some of my coworkers were nosy instead of observant.)

The site that I was located at consisted of a lot of office space. I thought with all of that office space that the company had I could take as long as I wanted killing time and goofing off. That didn't work to my advantage seeing that the tenants had a close eye on the security guard there. If something didn't look right to the tenants up there, they wouldn't hesitate to call the security office, describing what was going on with us.

One thing that I saw so vividly that I didn't see anywhere in my life was the fact that there were so many cubicles up there. I looked in amazement and thought, "Is this what people called their office?" For those of you that don't have any clue what a cubicle is, I will tell you.

(Please forgive me if you are working from a cubicle, but I have to explain it as true as I know how.)

A cubicle is an office space that is divided by several occupied spaces that appear to be a small office. It would be like a workspace with moveable walls on each side. The cubicle and the approach that one would have in mind would be an office.

The only thing about this statement that isn't true is the fact that the cubicle isn't an office, but just what it is, an office space. It is decorated with a computer, desk, and computer chair. Not saying this is bad, but what would keep one bound to this cubicle if they know that they can do better than a freaking office space? After I saw all of that I made a strong declaration that even these people, from the looks on their faces, don't like their job either. A few people that I saw up there that day exercised what appeared to be a genuine happiness about the cubicle life.

The cubicle life is the life that I describe that duplicates that of another life that at least 90 percent of us want.

Upon further investigation, from an eye-to-eye view over a period of some months, their faces that once had this glittery smile all of a sudden turned to gloom and sadness. Was it me, or were these people too experiencing the syndrome of the nine-to-five from a place that seems to be OK but in reality it isn't at all?

I didn't have to question myself too much longer; after about three months at this new security site, I saw with my very own eyes that the sad and gloomy-faced people were being replaced like old pieces of soap on the bathroom tub. At first this became a bigger surprise than I anticipated, not because they were gone, but because the office cubicle was still there replaced with another person.

When you sit down and have an honest talk with yourself about the job you work, you will come to the conclusion that no matter how far up you get, the cubicle will always be there waiting for her next occupant. Those of us that believe our worth is in what we have (remember that chapter) then will say that "as long as I can move to another cubicle I'm OK." To be honest, if we have to live just to be moved whenever for whatever, that's not much to live for.

The day that I witnessed those people moved from that office space, I also saw that young tall blonde hair guy talking on his phone again, this time from the seat of what looked to be an a executive chair. From my observation it looked as if he didn't have any worries. When the question came up about moving, it seemed that he wasn't going anywhere anytime soon. As I walked past this enormous office that took up about six or seven cubicle spaces, I could see vaguely that on his desk read in big bold letters **"CEO."** To me that is a major difference from the cubicle. That was the only thing that I could remember. That's the only thing that mattered to him. (And to me as well.) What is so exceptional about this man and his office is the fact that he is truly running things and things are not running him. Not only is he running thing from a boss position, he also has the ability to create other avenues of money just from being CEO of that company.

The people that we happen to deal with on a regular basis, whether we want to or not, are probably people that are trying to figure out how to get a raise, a better position on their job, suitable benefits, and other additives that will somehow boost them into success. It doesn't matter how long it takes, they just want to experience all of this so they can say they are successful. I thought that working up there in a space where you have your own cubicle with a computer and other things that make it look so adorned would be the best way to go instead of my security job.

Wrong answer! Any job that I have to bust my rear end and not have an option falls in the category right with the cubicle job. I remember one security site I worked at; my job duty was to stand in the front lobby of a huge executive building and greet everyone that walked in with a smile and a good morning. (As you all know, I disliked that job too; I thought whoever came up with that job didn't have a thinking capacity.) I got used to that pretty quick. I also got used to some of the same old slogans and greeting that the employees of the building would say to me each day. One of their daily slogans would be "Happy Friday!" or

"It's Friday!" Those people seemed to be so enthused about one day that it brought smiles beyond the sky to each of their faces. No one really appeared to be that enthused about the rest of the week, even with the rest of the week playing a big part in our lives. Those employees were living for that one day instead of the whole week since their jobs were not that great and enjoyable to them.

I believe when a person has the ability to sit in the executive chair then he or she has a habit of not living for the weekend, but to live for what they do. The cubicle lifestyle only gives you a normal lifestyle with normal outcomes. We all at some point in our lives tried to turn on that switch that would give comfort and an assurance that the person that sits in that executive chair is no different from the people who occupy that office space with those movable walls.

The fact is they are by far different and demonstrate it on a regular basis. This is something that is seen and not imagined; it has perfect implications that whoever sits in the executive chair has overwhelming ability to change where they are going and solidify their place financially.

The cubicle will always be there. There is no place in history for the person that has no desire to move from the cubicle and just continues to complaining, and always in a position that's questionable. The comment will occur that an open position is better than no position at all. Working somewhere is better than not working at all.

That may sound good, and thousands upon millions of Americans have enforced that theory, but at the same time, some seventeen thousand jobs were wiped out in the US last month. Professional service jobs—including those in finance, banking, and real estate—fell by eleven thousand, due largely to slowdowns arising from the collapse of the housing bubble and consequent losses in the financial sector.

Eighteen thousand government jobs were cut in January. The report notes that the number of jobs in the state-level education sector fell by twenty-six thousand last month. In the retail sector, apparel stores lost over nine thousand jobs, and department stores also reported decreases in employment. When I look at these statistics I grimace at the thought of what our work force is coming to besides a collapse.

Those of us that want to move from the cubicle to the executive chair must first acknowledge that the executive chair is always reliable, no matter what. There are very few executive chairs out there that don't make it. The turnover rate is that much higher between those moveable walls. (Remember, eighteen thousand jobs were cut last year among government jobs.)

The money that you lose from being cut out of a job is gained double or sometimes triple by those that sit in the executive chair, since they are the ones that generate their own money. The second thing that comes to mind when making this transition is figuring out what is your executive chair. The thing that differs most between the cubicle and the executive chair is the fact that you have a one hundred percent chance to change your life across the board when you sit in this seat of greatness called the executive chair.

No one can make that choice in your transition except you. It's out there for the taking; we have to change our pathways and place our feet on ground where the harvest is right. No one has to know that you desire to sit in the executive chair. That's for you and you only. And besides, we don't need anyone in our lives or around us that tell us that a cubicle is more suitable for life than the executive chair.

Chapter 12

Posses the Spirit of Entrepreneurship Daring to be different

When my mind finally got in line with my heart, I understood that creation concerning my life was great and should not be taken for granted by an immature thought that said I will work, work, and work until I reach my retirement age, and then things will be just fine for me.

I always wondered why it was so much easier to find peace and comfort in the cubicle lifestyle than in the executive chair persona. My answer came when I realized that the majority rules; those that collectively hold the answer to a question which somehow seem to maneuver and win over the minority, even if it is wrong and doesn't work for us.

The frame of mind that tells us so bluntly that we need to work is not the problem, but the problem lies when that same frame of mind tells us that the work is only the nine-to-five system from a collective group of people who have never done anything different from the nine-to-five. I think that puts a major damper on our creation as a whole, only excluding those who soak in the spirit of that executive chair and all the destiny that it brings to them. The rest of us are trapped by the long-awaiting death that the system will bring by way of a so-called retirement if we don't get out. Getting out is easier said than done, when the long life commitment between man and job has brought so much complacency to the mind of man.

Creation wasn't supposed to be anything like this, the feeling of false self-worth, controlled by the system, locked out from freedom by that imaginary door that stands in between poverty and entrepreneurship.

The physicality of a broken body bears the scorn of a domineering relationship that leaves you and me feeling empty, meaningless among society, while the system continues to lavish in their prosperous customs from day to day. From time to time I pray sincerely that the greatness in all of us will be distinguished from that that exhibits dissimilarity.

Most of my life I find myself isolated from most at times, not because I'm antisocial or emotionally attached to solitude, but simply putting it, there is a home for those of us that seek light in a dark place. I think that's the part of us that desires to be different. There is no light; everything is full of darkness. The "way we think darkness," "our commitment to the system darkness," "our hope of a better way but refuse to break-away from the cubicle's darkness."

There are a few of us that believe that the road to success is not your everyday nine-to-five system, but a street of stony rock that along the way may cause a lot of rejection, self-denial, misunderstanding, and more than anything a will to practice distinctiveness.

Theodor Adorno said it best with one of his great quotes when he said, "For a man who no longer has a homeland; writing becomes a place to live." This is a great example of the solitude that Adorno demonstrated that produce his great philosophical thinking, that without his differences in himself, he may have never been one of the ones that were able to go the distance in his desire for his own destiny.

At times in the past when things didn't go the way that I expected them to go, I doubted why I was created and dwelled heavily on things and people that are so common to me. The young lady that I speak with on a deeper level every time that we are on the phone or in person recently talked about change, and she voiced her belief in her own respectable way.

She talked carefully concerning me and my commitment to my isolation during several of our dinner dates. "Michael, you really don't seem to be here. You need to loosen up and be free. I want our friendship to grow; I want to know all about you."

I laughed while giving her a explanation, first making it plain that being different is the key to where I need to go in life. Then secondly I made it clear to her that I am who I am by God's creation, and I cannot change to be like someone else or something that I'm not. I was there but my mind was in a place of distance, a place of exploration, not of anyone else but of myself.

My mind stretched out a little, but not too far to where I'm out of touch with myself. I am fully persuaded that when you dare to be different in the face of the system, then your mind starts to free up to the point of desiring a distinction in your life.

I never take for granted the conversations that I have with this young lady by any mean; she is a close friend and her opinion about me does matter. When the dust settles and the smoke clears I still have to come to grips with who I am, no matter what people think about me.

In the world of the nine-to-five it doesn't matter at all who you are, you're longing to someday be independent; not having the system as a crutch on which we depend on daily for all of our money needs. In creation, we are so different that even our fingerprints never duplicate another in this world. So if that's the case, the number of people that are independent, free from the nine-to-five system, should be more than what the current statistics say. As reality has the final say, we are not as different as God has intended on us being since creation.

Going back for a moment to the last chapter, we found out that there are more of us that live the cubicle life than find greatness in the seat of the executive chair. In the true and honest heart of most, they find that life doesn't have to move away from their current situation, but instead just flow in the direction that it's going in as long as this train doesn't stop. For seventeen thousand Americans the train has already stopped, parked, and is at a stand-still.

For 87 percent of Americans, they prepare their whole lives to enter a job that they hate. For them as well, the train has stopped. The aspiration that we have for this train to keep pushing is a broken dream since it is designed to stop and in return disappoint us beyond measure. It not their fault that they terminate us, decline us from receiving a raise that we know we worked hard for. It's not their fault that they promised us a higher position within the company, then after some time we never get that position for some reason or the other.

The desire should not be to coexist with the system by desiring raises, job position, or time off, but our desire should be to exist in a realm of life that doesn't call for that, but gives us a seat above all of that. We feel that all that is linked to a higher life within the system is our security blanket and our way out. If that is the case we wouldn't be struggling from point A to point B within the system.

For so many years we have worn the coat of the system, taking away our uniqueness, making us just another person who is never willing to dare themselves to be different. Being different when referring to the system is making a few changes, and one change would be trading in those attributes that tie us to the system and put on the coat of an entrepreneur.

This by far is the biggest weapon that one could have against the system. This is the start of becoming different. From beginning of time all the way into the twenty-first century there have been many people, thousands upon thousand, that have from nothing dared to be different and in return have profited greatly from it. I believe that the first thing we must learn from this word "entrepreneur" is that it is universal. (Anyone, small, tall, uneducated, with no college degree can acquire this coat.) An entrepreneur is totally different from those who are system workers. Here is a brief definition in my own words.

First definition: you are not an entrepreneur if you are depending on a paycheck from week to week. Second definition: you are an Entrepreneur if you can lie in your bed as long as you desire, never getting a call from someone who says you're fired, and on top of all of that, somehow you receive money that generates fluently in your life and is working (money) while you sleep! This is hard for anyone to fathom when their lives are so full of everyday habits that they wouldn't know the difference if it fell from the sky hitting them in the head.

Let me clear up a statement that recently has been presented to me strongly by someone who claims that they are an entrepreneur before we go on. The statement went like this: "Michael, everyone isn't going to be an entrepreneur; some people are going to have to work for a living. Just because you want to be one and don't want to work doesn't mean everyone else will listen to you talk about that."

I was at dinner with this women, so I used a little bit of wisdom instead of foolishness so that our day in the park wouldn't be a night of living hell from what I would secretly call a major disagreement. To everyone who has been told this statement before, or perhaps who have said it on accident with no thinking (I'll give you the benefit of the doubt), let me be the first to address it. First and foremost, everyone and somebody are two different entities. "Somebody" refers to the singular person, and "everyone" refers to the collective group of people. So what everyone does, that somebody will not because they dare to be different. (Sound familiar?)

Thomas Edison was somebody, Henry Ford was somebody, Aristotle was somebody—the list goes on. If they all decided that "everyone" isn't going to be an entrepreneur, then would we ever be speaking concerning their entrepreneurship? The answer is no!

So next time this subject comes up, it won't be ignored by you or someone else not replying against it privately with what I just written here. From books to magazine to billboards to conversations, mention of entrepreneurship is spoken like everyday discussions with you and your best friend.

I believe entrepreneurship is something that is thought about seriously but pursued from a visualized state of mind rather then a physical action. A lot of us claim to be that of a entrepreneur framework, but when the rubber meets the road it turns out to be a different story. It's like running a presidential campaign: you have about five to seven candidates from each side that starts the race, and as the race goes on, you find some of those candidates that spoke so persuasive about what they will do to change America start to drop out.

That's how many of our so-called entrepreneurship minds operate. I will be the first to admit, becoming an entrepreneur is quite difficult, and at times you just want to flat-out give in and throw in the towel, mainly because it brings you to a point in life where you are giving (investing) more than you're receiving, and at the end you feel as though you are left with nothing. Reverting back to <u>Theodor Adorno</u>'s prolific quote, "For a man who no longer has a homeland; writing becomes a place to live."

This is a dividing point between the cubicle and the executive chair. This one quote tells me that Theodar Adorno "Homeland" mentally was lost, but his desire to create writing out of his own self meant a rest haven for him and in return became his new home.

A key point to learn: the spirit of an entrepreneur can be isolated and solitary that may end in some lost, but on the back end of it, you're exercising something that most people won't do and that's perseverance. Perseverance is the work of entrepreneurship. It is clear that Adorno was out of his comfort zone, but nonetheless, he made it comfortable with his perseverance. I would be willing to bet that more than a few people didn't understand him, nor were they willing to activate the necessities it took to find out. So in conclusion, we label him as being weird, self-centered, closed-minded, and perhaps crazy.

One thing that I have learned in my thirty-four years of living is that if a person doesn't quite understand your approach, they without a doubt will discredit your professed destiny that hasn't happen yet. To overcome this you must do what Adorno did, and that's finding what he calls a homeland (a comfort zone) in whatever you're trying to do that's going to launch you into entrepreneurship. For me, I believe that is a great diagram to go by when the odds are stacked against you.

It doesn't say that the odds were stacked against Adorno, but he says for a man who no longer has a homeland; writing becomes his places of residence. Whether Adorno was speaking of himself or another person, in the figurative or literal sense, or referring to writing as an appropriate approach for his entrepreneurship, he was right on point with his beliefs.

I am totally persuaded that with his various works that he achieved in his life, he had a plan along with others of his time, before him, and even now in the twenty-first century. There are a few things that demonstrate the spirit of an entrepreneur, and I would like to go into them before our time together in this chapter is over. I am won over with believing that these demonstrations of Entrepreneurship not only will help us, but also will give us hope in reaching our stature in becoming posed with the spirit of an entrepreneur and finally beating the system for good.

The first thing you must have is vision. It is virtually impossible for anyone to have any life form of an entrepreneur if they don't have vision. Someone told me some time ago that he believes he is going to be wealthy one day by becoming an entrepreneur. My response was, "That's great. How are you going to do that, if you don't mind me asking?"

"I really don't know Michael, but I just believe God is going to do it for me one day," he said speaking clearly into the phone. Although the state lottery is alive and well and some are lucky enough to win it, life as a whole isn't that lucky, so we're going to have to have more of a sensible way then he has in becoming an entrepreneur than just receiving it from God.

Vision is such an important requirement for entrepreneurship that if you don't have it, it would be like having a Mercedes Benz in your driveway and not having the keys to drive it. What am I saying? You can say that you are an entrepreneur or desire to be an entrepreneur but don't have a clue on how you're going to get there; well, it does you no good. You have a nice Mercedes Benz in the driveway, but no way of driving it simply because you don't own the keys to it.

What is vision? Vision is foresight that one has that will unlock the door to one's destiny. It's not just a thought or a desire that causes us to wake up suddenly while being wet with sweat; it is much more provocative then that. The idea of a thought or a desire with some of us is that it's all that we rely on and nothing else; we expect the desire or the thought to do it for us by unfolding our success for Entrepreneurship while we ourselves don't know. By no means am I saying that a desire or a thought won't lead us to becoming an entrepreneur, but wouldn't it be better if we had a blueprint, a plan, a design outline for our life by way of foresight that we can capture? One thing that I found to be true is that vision is far more reliable and in-depth than a thought or a desire.

Just think: when you apply vision over thought and desire you have given yourself a demand on yourself that will in return give precise foresight into entrepreneurship. The second key that demonstrates the spirit of an entrepreneur is called mission. What is mission? Mission is foresight working to come to pass by way of collected ideas from the vision and put into action. Let me set the record straight with what I am about to say. Listen closely; there isn't a possible way that we can have a mission without a vision. (I know that I will be receiving a lot of email for that statement, so my mission is to welcome them all!) Mission is like the driving force of vision: once your vision is up and intact, then you can have action that depicts your vision. For example, if your vision for your life is to become a store owner, your mission would be to get an understanding about certain products that will go in the type of store you visualize yourself owning, how much money it will cost to purchase the store, and temporary loans that you may have to take out to make your vision that much more genuine to you.

That is just one of a million examples of how a mission plays a vital part in your vision, having a way to walk and operate in one's life. Once again, it's not enough for one to have a thought that brings their mind into entrepreneurship, or a desire that staggers our performance for a time or two, then we're right back to living the normal, boring, and unproductive lifestyle that the system brings us.

We need precise keys that will play out over a course of time, not a standard of living that's suitable for the system but burdensome for all of us that are bound by it, and with vision and mission this is a major blow to the foundation of the nine-to-five system. Next in line after our mission is working, operating strongly in our life; we need persistence. What is persistence? Persistence is seeing the vision, and then working it through the mission no matter what may be up against you. This is the making or breaking of some, the divider between different and similar, those of us that want to continue the nine-to-five and those that want to sit in the executive chair. Persistence is the carrier of your vision and mission; this will determine how far you will get in your quest to become an entrepreneur.

Thomas Edison illustrated persistence in one of my favorite quotes when he said, "I have not failed, I've just found ten thousand ways that won't work." Benjamin Disraeli, the prime minister of the United Kingdom in the late eighteen hundreds and also a novelist, said, "The secret of success is constancy to purpose."

Dale Carnegie, a developer of famous courses such as self-improvement and public speaking, enlightened us on what defines persistence when he himself quoted, "Most of the important things in the world have been accomplished by people who have kept on trying when there seemed to be no hope at all."

In my understanding concerning persistence, these are the three most powerful quotes that I read that have been beneficial in my life thus far dealing with persistence. OK, let's put this third key in some comprehensive perspective. Persistence is a vital key in obtaining the spirit of entrepreneurship. It's essential because it tests your will to be an entrepreneur, and to work persistently when all hope appears to be lost and you don't have a chance in the world to bring your vision to pass.

Entrepreneurship is an ongoing work in progress. I will say that again so we can all get it: entrepreneurship is an ongoing work in process. This is not for the weak at heart, nor is it for people that want to give up and quit along the way. Benjamin Disraeli, Thomas Edison, and Dale Carnegie I'm sure experienced some difficulties along the way to what each of their visions consisted of. The third key works to perfection, making all of these great men an eternal headline and a model for those of us that don't care about a slump, a roadblock, a collapse in our own vision that hopes to keep us hopeless staying attached to the system.

But instead of a long life that doesn't make headlines, that doesn't bring men and women into entrepreneurship, these men grew in their vision, showing all of us that read about them that persistence is an imperative key in their quest to be different. The fourth key is just as important as the other three that we have talked about thus far, but not talked about a lot when associated with entrepreneurship. This fourth key in obtaining the spirit of entrepreneurship is called initial responsibility. I am somehow convinced that the reason why the job industry is so overcrowded with people who are supposed to be in the executive chair, instead of the cubical, is simple: they will not take the initial responsibility to change that scenario.

If we actually believe that everyone that is working a nine-to-five job right now is really supposed to be there forever and a day, then we believe that. Entrepreneurship really doesn't exist, it's just a thought that comes and goes. What is initial responsibility when referring to entrepreneurship? Initial responsibility simply means that we are totally liable for making all the keys in entrepreneurship work.

That's a tough one, right? So many times we say, if I only would have started two years ago, if I didn't have all of these kids, then maybe I could go back to school and get my degree in political science. If I had the money then maybe I wouldn't be in this position that I'm in right now that's holding me back. If you helped me like I told you to then my life would be a whole lot better than it is now.

All of these are examples that we come up with that keep us from obtaining the spirit of entrepreneurship. I believe that we think that the vision that we have to become entrepreneurs also belongs to the next person, and the man across the street, or our close relative that we have depended on for everything for most of our lives. That's not the case. It belongs to us, not them, so why should they be held responsible?

Most of the time, during our peruse of entrepreneurship, we get weary and fall by the wayside thinking that waiting on our situation to get better will advance ourselves. Thomas Edison knew very well that he was responsible for who he would become in his quote that says, "Everything comes to him who hustles while he waits." That's initial responsibility, that's the fourth key in our quest to possess the spirit of entrepreneurship. No one made Thomas Edison an entrepreneur; his desire for vision and his initial responsibility was to do something when that something wasn't working totally in his favor all at once. Nevertheless, through initial responsibility, Thomas Edison saw entrepreneurship working in his life; he was commented to a response even when things were not good for him and what he was trying to do. Edison is pointing out that if you actually do something to achieve your goals, rather than sit back and wait for your dreams to come to you - you are far more likely to get what you want. He worked initial responsibility to the fullest.

Many times in my life I have experience loss, so much loss it seemed unbearable.

I couldn't tell you how much it hurt to be hurt by people in and out of my life that I felt should have helped me in my time of what I believed was a crisis. Little did I realize that in order to see a crisis diminish, I had to do something and do something quick.

In early 2004, I activated the fourth key in the spirit of entrepreneurship and I didn't even know it. I was taking the initial responsibility to push past my frame of mind that told me, on a regular basis, that the dead-end nine-to-five system that I was working was all I had to look forward to and the struggle that I am in because of the nine-to-five will always haunt me the rest of my life. Now this fourth key didn't work itself in my life immediately as I thought it would, but it was working and that's all that matters.

Let me just add this: if we expected someone to help us, then that is the first unnecessary disappointment we may pick up and face in this path to entrepreneurship. The preliminary dependability to see entrepreneurship take place and work effectively in our life falls on us, not on anyone else. We thank God earnestly for their assistance and we don't take it casually, but we are so consumed with visions for our life we have taken the initial responsibility to make it work and not anyone else to make it work for us. (Remember that.)

The fifth key could have been the first key if vision wasn't the foundation of entrepreneurship; instead it takes its rightful place since a lot of people won't bend a little to make their vision come to pass. This fifth key is called risk. What is Risk? Risk is doing something out of the ordinary that's not convenient for you to make the vision come to pass, but in return it may cost you a decline or loss in the process.

Once again, this is a perfect place for this key in entrepreneurship. In order to truly become an entrepreneur (in my book), you have to be willing and ready to take risk. I'm not speaking from a book I read or a fancy thought that I conjured up, but I am speaking from a voice that has experienced it. This is one of those keys that either you do or you don't—there isn't any in-between simply because it has a twofold outcome.

If we are chasers of Entrepreneurship, then risk for us may be difficult but not out of reach by our flimsy thinking that says we can do without the risk taking. But in taking the risk (whatever it may be) to become an entrepreneur, then the chances of a positive outcome is greater than not taking the risk.

The second outcome may be that you don't see anything great at first but when you feel as if you had enough of your efforts comes the harvest. Those are the two final scenarios or the outcomes we face, those of us that really want to be a part of this long ride called entrepreneurship.

This fifth key, once activated, will prove that we are people that won't turn a deaf ear to the challenges that come along with the territory. This fifth key, when it starts to speak, when it demands for a higher walk toward Entrepreneurship, we won't over-talk it with our simple-minded thinking and our unchanged approach; no Entrepreneurship is just that intense, it's just that difficult once this fifth key is put into action.

Many before us has held this fifth key. In spite of disadvantages, they stood by their passion experiencing the risk it took to see them come forth. Now it's our turn, giving a chance to break free from that dark cloud that hangs over our head keeping us bound to the nine-to-five system. It is overshadowing what God has instilled in us from the very foundation of the world, but we won't waver making the fifth key to no avail, but we welcome it, making it a vital key in entrepreneurship. We have what it takes to make a drastic change, modification in our everyday activities that once left us hopeless and without risk; we suffer badly from this, but we come around to see this fifth key not as a stumbling block but a rise to occasion, and a spot beside those greats that demonstrated risk in their path to greatness and entrepreneurship. When I started to write my first unpublished manuscript, I must have been the happiest peanut-head young man alive.

I didn't have anything but a vision, a notebook, and a pen that hardly worked at the time; after I wrote a couple of lines and found them to be OK, I took them to a close coworker of mine. She thought the few lines were good and encourage me to write more. As I continued to write over a period of years, I finally manufactured the manuscript to a completion only to be disappointed by the publishers in not getting a book deal. Even though I felt a sudden distance from my writing and wanted to give up badly, for some reason I bit the bullet and pressed through all the disappointment, the rhetoric slanders that I face from people that weren't going anywhere but back to the nine-to-five. Now, sitting patiently in front of my computer screen, I realize that I possess the spirit of entrepreneurship and I didn't know it. The fifth key was alive and working in my life, and with that said, when you take a risk toward reaching entrepreneurship, you take major steps away from the system while taking a step to being an entrepreneur.

Losing my job, living at home with my mom, child support at it highest, instead of paying bill I gave close to fifteen hundred dollars to a publishing company that I didn't know for sure would help me in my publishing dreams or hurt me, I never wavered a bit but instead allowed the fifth key to work. (Thank God)

Finally we have made it to the last key, but we haven't reached the minds of those that read this book, if they still have a consistent belief that entrepreneurship is only for a certain race of people, certain genders, individuals who have everything going in their direction, seeming to be perfect in all that they do. For those people then, this book availed nothing with that kind of thinking. The downgraded rhetoric that I heard over the years and even recently concerning the thought of killing the thought, that the nine-to-five syndrome is the only acceptance of opportunity that one has at the moment to advance and move forward in life, is the sixth and final key in possessing the spirit of entrepreneurship.

Acceptance, what is acceptance?

Acceptance, when related to entrepreneurship, simply means to embrace all the shortcomings, all of the great moments, and every last inconvenient timeframes that act as though they are keeping us at bay. The truth of the matter is that from the ground up, entrepreneurship as a whole can be very, very, difficult to obtain right at once or in it fullest form, so to combat that thought that may come shooting doubt in and out of our minds, we have to accept the fact that it may be later than sooner before all of those positive and negatives are ironed out and we see the end result of what we envisioned from the beginning.

I don't dare to end this chapter without making it clear to you that acceptance is the core of entrepreneurship; it is the wall where all the other keys hinge upon. I can't get away from the quote by Thomas Edison that sends waves of chills throughout my body when it comes to one desiring the indwelling of entrepreneurship. The quote, for those of you that may have missed it, goes like this: "I have not failed, I've just found ten thousand ways that won't work." Thomas Edison accepted the fact that what he anticipated to work did not, but that acceptance wasn't failure but ways that didn't work. I am so tired of people relaying the message to me that everyone cannot be entrepreneurs, but take on the weight and burden of the nine-to-five system and get nothing but low wages and a headache. Why do we continue to try the nine-to-five but refuse to try being and entrepreneur? I will tell you why. We can't accept the fact that it may not work, it was many before you who felt like this but nevertheless they pushed through simply because they had nothing to lose. That's your answer, push through anyway no matter where you are right now and just try it and see what you come up with.

Thomas Edison was so energized on the sixth key of entrepreneurship that he spoke of it passionately in the above quote. His failure may have been a failure but he spoke of it in such a way that it was look upon in an acceptable manner. That's what we have to do not in just entrepreneurship but in life as well and that is accepting those things that are for the moment until we can change them.

The on-the-job training that calls for preparation through our mission for vision will seem like forever and a day. But the time for us to advance completely is coming to grips with the process of daring to be different so that we can possess the spirit of an entrepreneur.

We declare wholeheartedly that entrepreneurship is upon us and we will access all six keys that will ultimately spell out greatness for us. I have struggled long enough, I felt the low end of the stick, the system has ruled long enough, and now we get our chance to activate six keys that will cut the cord that kept us bound to the system for month's, years, and for some of us the majority of our lives. No more; we have possessed the spirit of entrepreneurship and we will see the manifestation sooner than later.

CHAPTER 13

"Time doesn't have any friends; it just has a respected and un-respected group of people that walks with it on a daily basis."
- Michael Arnold

"It is such a thing called being too late."
- Barack Obama

The last chapter I dedicated entirely to six keys I believe will help all of us progress by wearing and living in the spirit of entrepreneurship. Not only am I convinced of this fact, I am 100 percent guaranteed that if these keys are mapped out, then the nine-to-five syndrome will be just a memory that we can share with loved ones and others that we come across in life. I am so passionate about the vehicle of entrepreneurship that I wrote an additional eight pages on the subject. (I thank you for bearing with me on this topic.)

It is more important that entrepreneurship be brought to the forefront and taught amongst us all than getting out of our beds going to the nine-to-five forever and not ever engaging in entrepreneurship.

If one feels as if he or she has no future if he or she doesn't work, he or she has no future if entrepreneurship is not at least looked at by that one in thoughts of trying it out first.

The cop-out proclamation today by those that are in and out of the nine-to-five system is everyone cannot be an entrepreneur. (And I have to keep reiterating this so that the nine-to-five syndrome can be pulled out and destroyed by the root.) Let me restructure that statement. Everyone is not an entrepreneur, but for everyone that pursues it completely with those six keys in mind, the nine-to-five syndrome will cease to exist in that person's life.

Entrepreneurship and a nine-to-five job, which just as I said earlier are two totally different elements like night and day, and are not equivalent. What you receive from positive latitude when it comes to entrepreneurship you will never receive in the system, and the negative you obtain from the nine-to-five system on a regular basis you will never have as an entrepreneur. For some odd reason, many believe that the issues we have that are imputed in us from months and years in the confines of the system can't be done away with.

It's like saying that since there is still racism in America, then a black person need not run for president, or because we fail in putting forth an effort in becoming better in what we do, then we give up. What about this one: since everyone in the world can't become an entrepreneur, what makes me think I can?

What makes me think that it's not for everyone if everyone hasn't tried it? We know that everyone is not going to try it for all sorts of reasons, and one of those reasons I believe is time. Time places a major role in entrepreneurship working for us, and time also plays a role in whether or not we disconnect from the system forever.

I hope to expound greatly upon the concept of time when connected with entrepreneurship, while we all get the necessary information that will lead us not to be afraid to leave the system once and for all, but to be ready to leave the system once and for all. It's strange how you can talk to people that are close to you or that you know extremely well and in that conversation you mention your desire for progression, you speak about your vision just out of habit, nothing more, that in that vision you believe passionately that entrepreneurship is imminent for your life. After those type of conversations, I understand completely, first, that people's desire to become different is insensitive, and second, that they are so far out of touch with entrepreneurship that the nine-to-five syndrome will always be their centerfold.

The solution that I have for conversations like that is to avoid them as much as possible. Entrepreneurship is too vital, too important, and most of all, too necessary for one to think of it as being not for everyone, and then we engage in that dialogue with ones who believe just that.

Time is too valuable for us to feel as though we are incompetent from a conversation that destroys the theory of entrepreneurship, but builds up the idea that the nine-to-five system is more important since a greater percentage of people are participating in it. Now then, the question arises to all that desire entrepreneurship after we have done away with those unproductive conversations.

The question that I ask myself is, "Do I look at time as a very important aspect in finally destroying the nine-to-five syndrome and walking into freedom, or take time for granted, believing in due time it will happen regardless of what I do and don't in pursuing freedom?" Before I go further in my convictions concerning this, I first have to address the fact of those that believe that time is an institute for you to do nothing.

Recently I spoke with a friend; she and I had planned to go to the movies. Upon a quick follow-up the next evening around six, to my surprise, she declined. She didn't decline because of prior engagements, or a sudden problem that all at once occurred. She rejected my offer for us to go to the movies simply because (in her words), "I want to be lazy and lay around the house." I must be perfectly honest here; I was disappointed.

I wasn't disappointed because of the rejection of us not going to movies. I was disappointed because she looked at me as not being as significant as I thought she saw me as being. The movie is a small part of the equation, so small that I could have gone by myself, but the point is I valued her friendship more than I valued just going to a movie. Now, I totally agree that she took who I am for granted believing to herself that I will always be there for a movie date. Why? Because, as we say it, maybe another time. I didn't get bent out of shape about it; I used it as a place in this book to help us see that time is neglected and not seen as important, just as I was with the movie ordeal. In speaking of the organization that God himself has created called "time," He was brilliant with this tactic in which mankind could operate from a base or a foundation that would indeed bring about a thing of positive or negative in their life.

This foundation called time, first, is eternal. The system knows that; that is the reason why it wants to generate as much money as possible just in case it goes through a negative stage like the stock market, in which it goes downhill in their business instead of a steady upward pace. Those that are employed by such a system and choose not to break out of it find themselves in time, not gaining, but struggling dearly from the laws that govern the system and keep those occupied employees in bondage. Time will never alter its decision to slow down or perhaps stop so that we can get it together. That's not its job.

In entrepreneurship, those that believe it's the only weapon we have to overcome the nine-to-five syndrome have to have a clear plan, an unmistakable vision of what it is we so desire to do that will slowly but surely dismantle the wall of the system that keeps our eyes closed to moving out of the system. I am so overtaken and swept away with a strong belief that being an entrepreneur is the only way to demonstrate who you really are. So instead of me discounting everyone with the statement that so many people are using now, and I quote, "Everyone can't be entrepreneur," I embrace the new statement that I mentioned earlier, and I quote, "Everyone is not an entrepreneur, but for everyone that pursues it completely with those six keys in mind, the nine-to-five syndrome will cease to exist in that person's life and it is a good chance they could become an entrepreneur." Time is the only device that we have to move our vision into all six keys; it acts as a vehicle, not as a crutch like some of us think. One way I found that to be true in my life was when I desired to do something greater than I had been doing only to find over a course of time that it wasn't taking place. I grew angry and tired of life as I knew it, but after I figured out that time wasn't waiting on me. I had to do something about that.

What I have been convinced of is that when we are able to conceive that time is a vehicle to carry entrepreneurship, there will be a dramatic change in the life of those who work everyday and have no clue what they need to do to break free of that job. Many will tell you it won't work; you have to wait until it gets better on your end before trying it, or they just don't do it that way; you will fail. I have heard it all. Those people may finally cease to speak those words to me after they see that what I'm pursuing is far more greater than their negative words.

Not only do they not comprehend the concept of self-hope, they also don't realize that time is moving away from them slowly as they do nothing. From the years that I can remember, childhood to adulthood, I found myself between the four walls of the church (most of the time not on my behalf), and in being there, you hear a lot of suggestions and ways you can change you life, which I find to be the best part of attending those type of services. Not only do you hear suggestions and life-changing words of inspiration, you meet people in the local church that believe the same way with a little to add to it.

One of those added on that I have heard from is, and I quote, "When it's your time then it will happen." That's another one of those statements that people use to become complacent in their fact to do nothing, while enduring a long-lasting blast from the system, which doesn't procrastinate. I am totally in harmony with the words that are put together to form a belief that says, "There is a time and place for everything."

That may be truth, since time gives and takes away, but if we don't discover entrepreneurship as who we are and not just for certain people, then time would be just like the moving wind in the autumn night. We will be waiting on something that never comes because we are waiting and doing nothing in the process.

Max Frisch knew the importance of time and how it plays a vital role in what he did in the 1930s up until 1970s. Max Frisch knew how vital time was because it showed in what he did. He didn't go with the quote that so many of us used that I just quoted earlier. He didn't believe that time would bring him to becoming one of the most influential Swiss writers of the twentieth century. He allowed time to work for him.

He formed a quote of his own, that when it comes to time, you have to make it work on your behalf. Here is his quote: "Time does not change us, it just unfold us." Contrary to what the majority says, every change we get, we have to keep fighting, keep moving forward, looking ahead, understanding that we are not so much a friend of time, but we just respected it to the point where we are doing everything we can to pursue something other then the system . During the years that I worked at a job (the system) I felt an urgency that something better was around the corner, even after my vision was posted all around the clock in my head, and what I felt was true. I thought over a period of time that feeling would turn into reality.

It didn't happen as I thought, but tore my desire inch by inch. Some say my faith in God was weak, others told me that maybe that wasn't what I am supposed to be doing. Thank God I didn't believe any of those people, because if I did I wonder, would I be here talking to you today? It wasn't that I believe wrong or it wasn't my time. I hadn't done anything to make anything happen, so I maintained a steady position that was comfortable to me even though I felt something better was around the corner. Well, that goes to show you that feelings and time don't go well with each other. (Well, at least for me it didn't.)

We may feel one way about something, and in feeling that way time should notice whatever we are feeling that day and act accordingly, but as we find out thus far, an accelerating vehicle keeps moving until it reaches it's destination. Max Frisch knew his destination wasn't so much of a time issue it was a vision issue. (Remember that?) Because Max Frisch had a vision, he had a mission, and since he had a mission, he had persistence, and since he had persistence he executed initial responsibility, the risk he took when he enrolled at the <u>University of Zurich</u> in <u>1930</u> to study German literature.

The sixth key, which is acceptance, was in effect when he had to suddenly abandon his studies there due to financial problems after the death of his father in <u>1932</u>.

Instead of giving up, depending on time to heal him before he could do something else, he started working as a <u>journalist</u> and <u>columnist</u> for the <u>*Neue Zürcher Zeitung*</u> (NZZ), one of the major newspapers in Switzerland. Max Frisch took into consideration how valuable time meant to him; he already knew before that that he was born to sit highly in the executive chair. He was a respecter of time.

I understand truly (if you have ever been in this situation then you know exactly what I'm talking about) that for some reason, whatever that reason may be, when you are rejected by someone, you wonder what the problem could be. It's not a fact that there is a problem with you, it's a fact that just like time, people don't think of you as being that important. That's why it is so imperative that a goal is set in each and every one's life to not just think of getting out of the system but to actually get out of the system.

As I spoke earlier, just to add to it, movies in my opinion are not that important to me since they come a dime a dozen, but the people you go to the movies with are because they are just that significant. (Side note: never let anyone portray to you that you're not that important. You are that important; if you weren't you would not be reading this book, and even more importantly than that, you wouldn't be pursuing a brand new life.) You would not want to get better in your life situations.

Just like you and I, Max Frisch had a lot of loss, with the death of his father and financial problems (that would be more than enough to give up and say time will fix it all). but instead he didn't see time but he saw opportunity, and with opportunity came a playwright, architect, a philosopher, and of course a novelist. For me this is a big deal; nowhere in his account do we find that he worked for the system. (Let me just make this clear as I did in an earlier chapter: if you work for the system right now and plan to get out one day to pursue entrepreneurship, that's all that matters.) Max Frisch saw time to be that of a revealer. Whatever we are in or associating ourselves with, time will tell on us.

The topic that I have to start the beginning of this thirteenth chapter with coincides with Frisch's quote. "Time doesn't have any friends; it just has a respected and un-respected group of people that walks with it on a daily basis." When I first arrived to embrace this thought, I had yet to start this manuscript, so I know in receiving this, this was definitely an afflatus moment for me. I was so grateful to receive it, I wrote it down and saved it on my hard drive and luckily it came in handy for this chapter.

When I read something, or a statement of inspiration, motivation comes to my mind. I'm eager to speak about it to some of my closest friends, but I find that for them it's not that enthusiastic, so I take it and I rehearse it to myself, excited to have it. When I study this quote that came to me like a friend that has accompanied me from the beginning of my life, I smile briefly knowing that some that don't believe in entrepreneurship won't believe in this quote. Entrepreneurs that have came and gone have acquired their freedom and their thing of greatness by just a quote, a line, a passage of words that come together to form an idea that no matter what happens on the negative end, they will always have a sense of hope that will overcome that doubt that has been sent out to keep them from seeing you for who you are.

Contrary to popular belief, we are a product of our hearts and not of time. Time doesn't bring me into my vision as some may suspect, but time is the agent that will either unwrap those keys to entrepreneurship, or as Max Frisch says almost one hundred years ago, unfold them. When going one-on-one with the proposal to myself that speaks of the system as a waste of time, I tally up my thoughts, my ideas, and most of all the six keys in entrepreneurship that always keep me in remembrance that I must be a respecter of time and not an insolence of it. I believe that people have the ability to do something about their crisis at their everyday nine-to-five; that's not the problem. The problem is that they fail to establish a covenant with time that says, "We are neither friends nor enemies, and in knowing this, I will respect you as a vehicle for my life, not disrespecting you in any way, but honoring you for what you are, knowing that, in the future, I will exercise all six keys that will, in return, establish my life forever as an entrepreneur." I call that "The Covenant of Man and Time." It is very important that we form this covenant mentally so that we as pursuers of the executive chair won't wonder why we still have a homeland in the cubicle instead of the executive chair. What we must learn and learn quickly is that time is not to blame for what you haven't done as a person.

We talked pretty openly in an early chapter on who we really are, and we made the conclusion that what you do will determine how far you get in this race out of the system. So if time is an element of transportation, then why do we blame it for what we haven't done, when all it is doing is what it has been created to do?

Time doesn't have to adjust—we do. Remember, time isn't losing anything, we are, if we don't walk with it in a respectable manner. The first way we can do this is to agree with the covenant. Before any covenant was established there was first an agreement. Your covenant doesn't have to be exactly like mine, but simpler in the fact that it demands that you know the characteristic of time. Let me make something clear here with this first step in the time covenant: being in agreement with it is not saying from your mouth that you are in oneness with it, but in word, form, and deed, applying it to every part of your existence.

After that is established, the second step is modifying. If you're anything like me you may find that very difficult to do when you have to change to meet the qualifications of time. Remember, we are adjusting to time, not time adjusting to us. I'm just sold on the fact that with the job industry on the rise, gaining more and more money annually, we wait on time to somehow give us a way to make money like that or to just get out of the system all together. It doesn't work like that, but if we somehow modify our thought concerning time, then that may become a reality for us. The third step in walking with time having a like mind is preparation. Preparation could have been a key in entrepreneurship, but I feel it would be better as a step in the covenant. In the pursuit to entrepreneurship, I have found that preparation is used not to be positioned for a letdown, but positioned to be lifted up, so instead of a whole lot of preparation I thought it would fit better when speaking of time. When speaking of time, I have to prepare for the time that I become an entrepreneur more than prepare steps that I will fail on this journey. I come up from under those things that may destroy my victory along the way.

The last step that I have is called comprehensive approach. This is the most important step one could have in the covenant of time by far. Not only does it work, and is a powerful step in walking with time, but it gives a true account on the character concerning the system and what it does to people.

Comprehensive approach means that I have, through hard work and adjustment, contained a complete outlook on how both time and I will cohesively work together on making entrepreneurship come to pass. To make a side note, I believe that the six keys to entrepreneurship are so influential that they will work once implemented, but if there isn't a covenant established somewhere after you receive the six keys, then you will depend more on time and not the ability that God has given all of us to make entrepreneurship work.

John F. Kennedy, the thirty-fifth president of the United States, confirms this with his quote that reads, "We must use time as a tool, not as a crutch." As we all have come to know, John F.

Kennedy accomplished so much in his lifetime, and his quote wasn't just hot air, but instead it was fundamental life to those that feel time is insignificant because it serves like a rotating door. But as time acts as that rotating door, who is to say that, when it comes around a second time, those six keys that we have for entrepreneurship will still be activated to open the door where that executive chair sits. Barack Obama made a stunning and powerful statement that is so in harmony with my account; his quote goes like this: "It is such a thing called being too late."

In quest for him to do something in his life that has never been done before, but in America, he understood how time plays a major role in it. Barack Obama knew that just because he desired to be the next president, that a certain time element wouldn't take him there alone, instead he used opportunity as his motivation by creating a presidential campaign and allowed time to move him to it through his own actions.

Speaking of time, this is so timely because it coexists with Kennedy's quote in the fact that we could see time as a crutch if looked at not as a tool, and if not look at as a tool even with the six key of entrepreneurship, you can be too late. They (friends, families, others) have said time and time again, "Why are you pursuing a book when you are behind in bills? Why would you spend close to twenty-five hundred dollars to get a book published when you could have used that money to catch up bills or a savings account?"

I never had a second guess that they possibly had a point; instead I told all of them that time is of the essence, if I don't do it now then I don't do it at all because I would be too late. I made it clear to all of them that I have made a comprehensive approach to time, coming to the conclusion that I adjust and not let time get the best of me. The time for entrepreneurship in our lives is now, not tomorrow, not the next day, but now. We won't flirt with waiting any longer, but we will establish a long life covenant that will read, "We are neither friends nor enemies of time, and in knowing this, I will respect you as a vehicle for my life, not disrespecting you in anyway, but honoring you for who you are knowing that, in the future, I will exercise all six key that will, in return, establish my life forever and I will see my destiny come to pass." With some of our thoughts we believe that as long as time exist then we have the chance to do whatever we fill that is our pursuit in life.

But as Barack Obama, Max Frisch, and John F. Kennedy were solely convinced upon with their quotes was the fact that when ever you are enlighten with opportunity, do it right then don't wait. Waiting through time could actually be the death of it and not life.

The reality factor may be that you have problems, we all do, and time doesn't heal your problems or even take them away you do with change. It is not so much about time but opportunity.

CHAPTER 14

The "Moment Entity"

A couple of things that this book has taught me as I spent hours upon hours working on it have been sincerity, integrity, and completeness. A lot of the so-called help books key in on people and point the finger at them and not at themselves. Sincerity in my belief in this book and in you, integrity because I am truthful in my belief and completeness because you and I stood the test of times to be who we were created to be.

In writing this type of book, I realized that it becomes vitally important that we don't get so caught up in boosting ourselves up (those of us that are writing the books) and putting the readers down.

The reason why I decided to write this book is for the readers, to allow them to know not that they are going downhill because they are a major contributor in the system. They already know that, but to relay the message that God relayed to me one day, and that message is, "I love you and things will get better in your life; here are the keys." If you are that person, I'm talking to you, I wrote this book for you, I stayed up late nights and early mornings for you, because you deserve to know that the nine-to-five is a syndrome that kills us mentally and physically. I know that, not because I thought it up, but because I went through it between the ages of about seventeen to thirty-four off and on, so now I can present it to people like you that are willing to accept it. That's important to me; I call it being transparent.

It's not about a paycheck or the highest position on the New York Times bestsellers list, but what's imperative is knowing that when I go to bed at night, and people read this book, there is some necessary information that they will read that they now can apply to their lives and sooner than later kill the nine-to-five syndrome.

In my thoughts and my everyday living, this is the most humbling experience that I have ever been a part of—not just writing something you read or perhaps a situation that someone else gone through, but you yourself have seen all the bad and negative attributes that have attacked on a daily basis. Even now as I sit here patiently at my uncomfortable computer desk and my cushioned seated chair, physically I sit here with aching pain in my small-framed body.

Somewhere between me starting this manuscript and about ten thousand words close to being finished, I endure this pain from a temporary job that I took in order to take care of some of my financial issues. I said it earlier that if you have to take a job as part of your vision, do it, but understand that it is temporary, and the more you see the desire to change that, the more you see yourself out of the nine-to-five syndrome. As I endure this physical pain, I also battle with all the complication that comes with every attempt to get out of the system. It is not an easy thing, but it is doable when you have come in contact with your life as it really is, then realizing that we must exercise those keys, those of us that want to see greatness through entrepreneurship. Now, with this moment, it says that with all the pain and all the negative sidetracks that I find myself enduring, somewhere down the line things will change. That moment that covers and protects me from myself may prevent me from prevailing and moving to a place in life that I have never been. In going to this place, it brings completeness to your life that you may be able to witness that you stood the test, didn't give in, and held on to see it manifest. That's the sincerity that we have to have to progress, to see something different in our life. From the year of 2004 to this present year, I have been consistent in my faith to become the best writer that I could be in the midst of the physical and mental pain that I have endured in the last four years.

No matter how much (at times) that my mind wanted to stop and my body wanted to say this isn't the way to go, people don't care to hear you, there was something great that kept me at bay, something that told me to keep going. It had something to do with the extension of my life and what it would become.

After I came in contact with a moment, I had to have something that would carry it, keep it alive, wear it, and walk every aspect of the moment out to perfection. The diagram of my life wasn't ever set up to be unflawed and without defect, but instead it was the total opposite, containing misfortune, defeat, and much disappointment. The disappointment was so great it was hard for me to have a mind outside of the diagram that I saw with my physical eyes. (It is easier to see something negative that's tangible and believe that than observe the positive, unseen and believing that to come to pass.)

With the diagram of my life from my perspective being a total screw up, I found myself fighting for my life, hoping that somewhere down the road my existence would change and my days on earth and it would not be in vain. The fact still remained that the nine-to-five syndrome was alive and well, working against anything that would bring that best out in a person. But from the hinges of a moment, things begin to change for me; the diagram that laid out my life wasn't really that bad.

My life, which was confined by the system along with my own personal problem outside of the system, started to correspond with what I call the "moment entity." This is when the opportunity came out of nowhere for me to do something about the hell in my life from the nine-to-five syndrome that gripped me at the time, a sixteen-year stranglehold on my life. A moment entity is the opportunity to change the diagram of your life in an instant by way of an entity. Although a moment is part of time, it is slightly different. A moment speaks of right now, a flash, an instant, today. Time speaks of tomorrow, era and in many terms generations; it is the vehicle that carries this moment or opportunity when I refer to "moment."

I wasn't sure if the moment entity was enough of a push to subdue the problem that I felt everytime I went to work each day of my life. For years my life tallied numerous thoughts and incidents that wouldn't give me an outlook outside of the system, so I felt as if I was stuck. My past was unpleasant; certain events caused a strain on my belief for a better future, and a complete me now knows that for the lack of respect and a non-convent with time it had unfolded me, showing my disrespect for it.

I knew whatever I could do to get out of the situation of going to a job that all I had to look forward to was social security and a retirement plan in thirty years, I had to do it. If you would break down my term, moment entity, it would be that the opportunity to overcome the nine-to-five syndrome coming to me in bodily form. On the job that I worked at the time (security), I met a young lady from Africa. We had something in common, and that was conversation. We talked about various things the more we saw each other.

One of the main things that our conversations consisted of was getting out of the work environment once and for all. As the conversation reached its peak, I felt like crying when she said what she said to me that day, standing in a building parking lot working a security post. She said, "Arnold (we were addressed by our last names), this is not where you want to be for the rest of your life. God has something else inside of you that is far greater than this. If I can come to America and not know any English and pursue a degree in chemistry, you can get out of here! God cares about you, and he doesn't want you working here forever. I couldn't speak, Arnold, but I said to myself I would try until I could." "I wanted to know English."

"You're right, Yemi." I responded with tears in my eyes.

"I'm serious, Arnold. One days in the future I don't want to see you in here, but where God wants you." After the supervisor called her back up to the main desk I was left to ponder, thinking and breaking down that conversation.

Yemi's words were the "moment entity" in my life that completed the words that I thought on a day to day basis that said boldly that a better job is what I have to aim for, a better job will launch me into the place where I need to be, a better job! I dwelled on her words; I moved accordingly, viewing her as a place of rest, fresh air for those who were weary and struggled to move in hope. She became that for everyone and not just me.

God had indeed given me a second chance at life at the age of twenty-seven, and for that reason and that reason only; I believed that something would change.

I worked overtime, trying to figure out what it was that made me significant, what it was that not only would one day free me from the nine-to-five syndrome, but would give something to others just as God had given me in the "moment entity." It was just a thought, a feeling of excitement, with zero action. My problems in my personal life kept growing while the diagram of my life stood at a big flat nothing.

The boat that I was in wasn't that bad. I was working, the pay was OK, and I could get extra hours, so what was so bad about that? No matter how many of her words counteract my thoughts, I was not willing to kick against them to at least give myself a different outlook on life.

"Hi Arnold, how are you today?" She spoke so calmly like she always did, nothing changing. I wanted to walk away. I didn't want to hear a word that she had to say, not because she wasn't right, but because the opportunity to change the diagram of my life seemed more difficult than just doing what I have been doing which was nothing.

I admire Yemi to the utmost; her words were words of life and healing and overcoming from a future standpoint. I wanted to grab them, but I wasn't willing to get out of the boat. "I'm doing OK, Yemi, are you?" I gave her a short smile. I knew the night before I was involved in things that didn't give me any hope, made her words of non-affect in my life, and for that reason after a long while I felt as though this is it.

That security company, not having the love that I felt I deserved, a certain mindset that wasn't positive, not seeing any change in my life, believing something great one moment then not believing it the next moment. The diagram that I saw was the diagram that I believed. "I'm doing OK, Arnold, I'm just a little tired. I went to school and I had to be here and I just got a little sleepy." "That's good that you're in school and working, Yemi." "I'm trying. God is giving me strength in all of this and I thank him a lot, Arnold, if it wasn't for Him I don't know what I would do." I shook my head, letting her know that I was in agreement with her; she smiled while she talked and I responded accordingly. Her whole thought process was going into a direction in words that I expected but didn't want to hear because I knew it would challenge my will to change my diagram.

"to be continued"

CHAPTER 15

Passing the Keys of Entrepreneurship
(The Meshach and Camden Years)

I want to take a few minutes to catch a quick breath, relax for a moment, let that digest, and go back to it. Not you, but someone else that's reading this book, may say, "Why in the hell would he stop and put a "to be continued" statement in bold at the end of a chapter when he could have continued on the next page?"

Well, I would be so glad to answer that question. When I write I write from the inside out and not from the outside in, so my writing is so heart-filled and not secular driven that I have to go the route of my heart, and my heart has taken me to a halt, a pit-stop, going to fill up for gas, but we have not left our point of destination. I can hear someone say, "Stopping for something important, like taking the children to the restroom at a convenience store or a nearby restaurant."

Now you get it, that's exactly what I'm speaking about. Just a pit stop (an important one); we have not dismissed our destination, we're still on that road, hang tight. If you have any children, or you know any and you can get to them at this moment, or perhaps any of your relatives may be children, grab them up now or read this chapter to them sometime soon, because this is for them.

Somewhere between me working voraciously in the system and

discovering the six keys to entrepreneurship, there was an addition to my life, then a recent addition that I didn't expect, that kind of popped up and entered like it was there all along. That sudden pop-up was two children.

Both are boys, thirteen years old and sixteen months old, who I love dearly. And not just for them, but I write this chapter earnestly for all children that will come after me, to revolutionize their paths tomorrow by what we lay down for them today. Several chapters before this one, I wrote concerning legacy and how important it is to those of us that are not just passing through. In my thinking and reasoning, legacy is vitally important to me simply because my two sons Meshach and Camden are following in my footsteps.

Who do you have following in your footsteps? Think of it like this: if you have a good friend who you care for in a deep, deep way, so deep that you would keep him or her out of harms way, you relay to him or her anything that would help their life, or if there is something that you have gone through that has been a major downer in your life and you see this friend going that same route, you would warn them. Right?

Legacy is the same way, sort of, except you are preparing your child's path instead of that friend so they can carry on what you have established. You are preparing their path so they can avoid the stumbling block and prepare for their children, it's about generations. Something that we must learn and establish upon the table of our heart is that entrepreneurship is the expression of legacy. For all of us who are entrepreneurs who feel as if we have reached the highest that we can reach in our quest for entrepreneurship, try grabbing your child, or if you don't have any then go to some of the community where those kids would be the most appreciative of your time and educate them in the art of Entrepreneurship so they too can follow your path and you establish a legacy for them.

That's the upper level of Entrepreneurship that most people for some reason won't go. I spoke with my thirteen -year-old some time ago and asked him what he wants to be. He told me several things, from a professional horse rider to a police officer, he had a variety of choices, but one thing that I realize about his choices is that they change from day to day. He didn't just have one choice that he stuck with; he had several that he would tell me about that he wanted to be at one time. That's not bad, by any means, but the number one thing that I'm teaching my son as we speak now is passion. What is it that he or she likes to do anytime, anyplace, anywhere? That's their passion. The book of Proverbs, which means a whole lot to me when it comes to children, it says, "Train up a child in the way he should go and when he is old, he will not depart from it (*Proverbs* 22:6)." For lack of time I won't go in-depth with this Bible scripture, but I will touch on an important point. If it is my responsibility to raise my children, then it's my responsibility to raise them in such a way that the system is not an option and will never become an option under any circumstance for them.

When you teach your child as a child, that's the way that he or she will go (his or her path in life which is entrepreneurship); when he or she become an adult, he or she will not depart from it. Many feel as though this Bible scripture just means from a biblical standpoint and nothing else. The writer of the book of Proverb was trained up in the way that he should go by his father David, which was an Entrepreneur.

So David's Legacy was the writing of entrepreneurship for his son Solomon. There has to be a bridge between the children and entrepreneurship. What will bring them to entrepreneurship after you have done what you need to do as a parent? What keeps them interested after discovering their passion?

One thing as parents or as a person that has been assigned to lead a child into their destiny is that you have to demonstrate patience on all areas of the spectrum. I believe that most importantly when you have these precious people in your care, to protect their potential and seal them from all outside interference that may cause a sudden decline in their quest to see their own destiny come to pass. It is so easy not to give all that you have when you are dealing with a child or in my case my own children. David as a child was called to be king over Israel, and so his path was set accordingly, and accordingly may be doing things that the average person doesn't do.

When David played the harp giftedly before a king who despised him, when his heart was stronger then the strongest man named Goliath, that caused him to kill Goliath dead, and after that to sit on the throne as King. David wasn't just your average child, young man, or old man he was a person who knew his destiny.

So all my young children out there, no matter how much pressure you're under, no matter what negative words you get from friends, teachers, or whoever that you have to deal with in your life, you are not an average kid, you are a kid that has been created for greatness. Don't let anyone tell you otherwise.

There shouldn't be a word or words that come out of our mouths that say our kids will go to college, accumulate all that school debt, only to get a job that doesn't come close to launching our kids into destiny when they get out. The old term that I have been hearing for quite some time now is "lead by example," and I tell you, yes we have been leading by example.

Some parents (like me) may say, "I haven't been to college, so I don't have to worry about my child having to deal with college debt; I'm just a participant of the system and I want them to grow up to be better then me, they have that passion." Isn't that what we say as parents and overseers of our children?

The fact of the matter is they do have that passion and desire to be in a better position and reach destiny, so they're not using those of us as parents that work in the system as an example, but those of us that have already been where they're trying to go. Our children now find what they see to be an example, especially when considering college.

It's OK if we the parents or the guardians haven't been to school or desired to ever go, but what is vitally important is that we teach our kids patience by explaining to them the importance of passion and not debt.

According to the U.S. Department of Education, in 2005-2006 just over 52 billion school loans were provided for 6.5 million students in

America. Also, in 2005-06, federal student loans totaled an estimated $68.5 billion. About $57 billion in consolidation loans were also made in 2005-2006, as contrast to $44.4 billion in 2004-05 and $36.7 billion the year before. What is that saying? It's simple: this is the lead by example that our kids are seeking when we don't teach them the importance of a better way for their life. Education is the best thing when it comes to the advancement of our children, but it is up to us as parents to assure them that there is a better way for them then having this kind of debt coming out of college. I stress the point to those of us that are pursuing entrepreneurship, we need to do it now and not later. Three parts of that better way are passion, patience, and progress.

That is what I call the three demonstrations of destiny. This is what King David had then displayed in his life as a child in order to take his world by storm and influence his son Solomon. This is the better way that I have seen that can get children past the "lead by example" way of life for our children. Once again, if some believe that education is the only way in terms of destiny, then we in more ways then one deprive them of the chance to experience destiny from an entrepreneur point of view.

Education in terms of our children receiving more teaching and academics is good, but if there is a passion, a drive that is like no other, if our children isolates themselves, not as the spectators think, but as that child thinks, they can become better—not like the majority but like the minority.

Education no doubt beats not doing anything at all, and education is a force to be reckoned with when placed against nothing, but when the child cries in the darkness and his or her destiny lies at the footsteps of greatness, education is only added onto that equation of that big picture known as entrepreneurship. If my passion was that of an entrepreneur at the age of ten, eleven, twelve, thirteen, fourteen, or perhaps that age when I starting working in the system, where would I be at today? That's the question that I want Meshach and Camden to ask, not themselves, but me, who is the path for their life.

David started at a young age as a shepherd boy, and then grew into more of what his passion was, and that was to play instruments; serve in the kingdom of Saul; become a great writer, a successful soldier, and a leader of an army; and to finally reign many years as a king over Israel.

If we could compare David to anyone in today's time we would have to compare him to more than one person. He would be considered to be a very successful person in that he would be an instrumentalist, a writer that lived in the white house, a soldier, a military commander, and lastly a president.

It would be quite difficult to find someone who has all of these qualities in one. But as time moves and it stops for nothing, we find out in the confines of time that there are always children that grow up and wonder, and so just like Thomas Edison, they experiment with optimism and apply passion to that hope until those rare qualities that the majority doesn't have come to that minority. I have a friend who I have known for the last ten years. When I first starting writing, I made it clear to him that this would start and end my life as I know it. In other words, what I was telling him is that writing will be my start of success, and when I die it would be the end of my success and the start of someone else's, so that's why it is so important that I get started in doing what I have to do now to establish that for the next generation.

And that was four years ago. He told me of an idea that means the world to him (so he says), but there is no evidence that he is making an effort towards this idea. Another young lady that I speak with on a regular basis (just as much as my close friend) told me that I inspired her to write a book because she knows that's what she's suppose to do. This was about three years ago, and we still don't have a book out of her yet. To all my wonderful and inspired children and to all the parents and guardians that watch over them, this is what you don't want your mind to operate from; this is called procrastination. It's not enough that you have an idea or a mental image on how this idea with play and how you will benefit from it; you have to demonstrate all three exhibits that make up destiny.

All three demonstrations of destiny are exploits that expand our children and not just keep them with just a good idea sitting aimlessly in their heads. There aren't any excuses for procrastination. Why? Some would ask. If there isn't enough time for one to exercise this big idea, can't it be done at a later date? The answer is yes, but that's not procrastination. Procrastination is when that good idea or that passion that desires destiny and wants to see it come to pass by action but never comes to pass because we put it off until tomorrow, and tomorrow never gets here because we still live in today, that's procrastination.

Just like destiny, procrastination happens over a period of time, making it valid in one life. If you talk with these procrastinators you will discover that the bright idea that they have has originated from a young age in their life. David's idea to acquire six hundred men in an army started when he was a young boy beating Goliath in his first epic battle as a soldier. His desire to keep pursuing his life when the king of his own nation was trying to kill him carried him right to the throne.

David thought ahead. He knew that if his son Solomon was to at least desire any signs of greatness, he must have greatness as a billboard in his mind first. If there is going to be a "Solomon year," there first has to be a "David legacy." When people talk to me and we have these "conventional conversations" concerning entrepreneurship and these individuals are not on the same page as I am, it's not so much that they are wrong and I'm right, it's just that these conversationalists don't have a preexisting legacy that they can pattern their life after and so they have no confidence in the great year that can be in their life.

I used to be so disappointed, not just with them, but also in myself. I felt as though I said something wrong or I was being a little too pushy with my issues that often may have come out too bluntly, but as I mentally reevaluate them privately, I find them to be helpful to me and to a few others that are in my life. So in knowing that, I am a little at ease with their decision to disregard some of those passionate issues of mine.

David's legacy wasn't disregarded, nor was it something that was winked at by his fellow friends and acquaintances, but it was in fact a monumental event that changed the world that he lived in.

He turned the world upside-down with his desire to operate from this monumental stage. There are hundreds, maybe thousands, of children and their parents who are reading this book now who feel the same way; not just today, not just yesterday, but for years! You've been burdened with this indwelling on the inside to change the way you do things. It not a fuzzy feeling, but it's destiny flowing circumspectly up and down your body.

So many people try very hard working overtime to discourage our children from a place in life called destiny. A right place where legacy and entrepreneurship live, a place where they live and feel comfortable within themselves. This may seem abnormal to us as parents, and somehow because we are parents we call ourselves wanting to help them, but helping our children the most was when we accepted the gift, the passion, and the desire that's inside our children that God has given them.

In more ways then one, if we as parents find that we do this consistently, this will prepare our children to know and understand that the nine-to-five system won't shut them out of their destiny.

David was one hundred percent sure of this destiny thing, but his father Jesse wasn't. It is very important that we declare to our children that no matter how old they are, how much they mess up, or how bad their school grades are that they are still great, they are still winners, they are more than conquerors, they will become anything that they want to become, because we, the parents, said so!

That's important. Jesse (David's father) never told him who he was and what he would become. If so, Jesse would have had him present with his other brothers at the presentation for the next king of Israel. Instead David was forgotten like an important thought during an important conversation.

He didn't see his own son David being nothing more than just a shepherd boy, just a caretaker of sheep. But with greatness comes recognition. I have to be honest and straightforward, as I feel that I have been throughout this book (and I have to include myself in this as well): If we don't recognize our kids as being great, special, gifted, and full of destiny, someone else will.

We can look at that from two perspectives and get two different results from it. The first perspective is kind of like I said earlier; someone will see and take notice of the destiny inside of our children, and in whatever way they can they will pull our kids away from their destiny, whether with drugs and alcohol, street gang influence, premarital sex, crime of all sorts, jealousy, and one that affects us all: procrastination. (Telling a child that they don't have to pursue their dream they have their whole life to do it).

These are just a few of the fiery darts that get thrown at our children by those who don't want to accept and help our children walk out their destiny into entrepreneurship. (This is the first result.) Saul the king of Israel was sure of David's destiny after he killed Goliath before many people. Not only did he know of it, the people of the city knew of it as well. Instead of Saul doing whatever he could to assist David in pursing his destiny, his whole entire life he wanted him killed. But even in all of that Saul's son saw something great in David and because of it, as long as he lived he always helped David escape his father and helped him pursue his destiny.

Now, the two perspectives are total opposites. There are some of us out there that will almost die in order that others' destinies are fulfilled. The children that stand on the edge of greatness and feel free to express it when no one seems to want to look or hear you out: don't be afraid, go, pursue and conquer in the way that you know you should to express, to those few who will listen, that I want to do something different than the usual. Somewhere between parents and children, not hearing happens, and so therefore passing the keys of Entrepreneurship is lost amongst our inability to hear. Nevertheless, keep speaking. Someone will hear you.

One unlikely person heard David through his action. Jonathan, Saul's son, saw the greatness, the destiny that lay at David's doorstep.

He saw the keys of entrepreneurship (the ability to create something from nothing and call it your own) rest, ruling, and abiding in his life. He knew it was of the essence that he gave David a key that would be a major assistance in his life and would cause David to pass that same key later on in his life. This key that I am referring to is the key of friendship. One thing that is vitally important to our children today is that we help them, and teach them that having keys that unlock prosperous friendship will help them in where they need to be in life.

Jonathan was already a man that was fulfilling his purpose as a solider and a king's son, so what came with being both of those were provision. To all my children out there who are reading this book or to the parents that are reading it to them, if the friends that you (children) have in their life right now don't make a provision for them some kind of way in your life that's going to point toward your destiny, then you must question their friendship.

We cannot choose our mother and father but we can chose our friends, and before you (children) accept a key that doesn't unlock friendship but only animosity, God will lead those people to us with the keys that unlock friendship. None of us are an island or a planet that doesn't have any occupants; we need people to access us on this long journey that I call entrepreneurship. Something that I can say concerning myself is the fact that whenever I write, no matter how I write, and no matter how many books I write, if no one wants to read them then that's not helping me. I don't care if people buy them, what is important is that you read them—that's a whole other story! David was on his way somewhere great and Jonathon just wanted to help him. The friendship between David and Jonathon was so intense that they made a covenant between themselves. The covenant went as follows:

> *Then Jonathan and David made a covenant, because he loved him (David) as his own soul. And Jonathan stripped himself of the robe that was upon him, and gave it to David, and his garment, even his sword, and the bow and to his girdle.*

This is just one example of a friend that is a friend despite what he himself had to go through on his end to keep the friendship active. This is the first result of the second perspective that I spoke about a couple of sentences up. Although David went through some tremendous times in his life, he never got rid of the objects that kept him grounded, first, God, and second, his passion to live for God through his destiny. David accomplished a lot in doing this: slaying a giant ten times his size, becoming an armor-bearer for a king that wanted him dead, leading an army to many victories, and then finally becoming king and reigning there for forty years.

Jonathan as a remarkable friend did a lot for David while seeing this destiny unfold; not only was David influenced by this friendship, but others that came along the way as well.

David's mind stood out in the realm of destiny and waited for it to grasp the manifestation of this dream while holding onto the keys that structure this destiny. After David's time was up, after his accomplishments, his dreams, his many victories on earth, there dangling in the atmosphere were those keys of entrepreneurship. Now it was time for his son: the Solomon years to take hold of what David laid as a foundation for him.

That is such an important things to all of us that have kids, the desire we as parent have to allow our kids in on our destiny by handing them keys.

My mother is the best mother in the world and I could not ask for a better one, but as much as she been through as a child being blind from a careless accident and now an elderly women, she has no keys to give me except advice and for me that's just as good and I love you forever mom for that.

But where one is lacking the other is present. I have keys not just for my two boys but for your children as well, the keys that says no matter how bad it was for you, no matter how much people count you out, no matter if your childhood was scorn with a one parent home just as mine was, there is still hope; hope to dream, hope to be whatever you chose to be. Now take these key of destiny and change the world and turn it upside down for your life!

CHAPTER 16

The "Afflatus Moment"
(In Just an Instant)

The Solomon years superseded (in my opinion) the David years by far, mainly because of the Holy Temple that Solomon built during his forty-year reign as king over Israel. He did this and had a mind to do this because his father passed the keys of entrepreneurship to him before he died. Passing these keys to Solomon meant one thing, and that one thing was legacy being expressed by entrepreneurship. David had gained a lot of ground, popularity, and favor amongst the people, and beyond that he was the king over Israel. David himself had created the blueprints for the temple and desired greatly to construct it himself, but because God had a better way and David was adherent to God's plans, he had to give those plans to his son. This wasn't a letdown to him or a discouragement by any means, but in fact it was a blessing to him in that he had keys, an opportunity to pass them to Solomon—unlike David's father Jesse, who didn't have anything to pass to David except a desire to take care of sheep and produce offspring.

That's not to say that Jesse was a bad father, or a man that didn't have a desire to do better, but maybe David's moment to do better wasn't embraced by Jesse enough to do something about it. He may have been so out of touch with destiny that he didn't even recognize that his own son was destined for greatness.

This may be true, but what came up in the house of Jesse was a moment, an instant, a pathway that was covered with bumps and stumbling blocks, but at the very end that road smoothed out as destiny is reached. Our parents may not want to embrace destiny or feel as though entrepreneurship is for a certain type of person, but in a moment— repeat that to yourself, a moment—all in one moment, David changed his father's views, or any of our views concerning the will to create something out of nothing, and built something great all in a moment.

Many people that I speak with about their current position in the nine-to-five, when I relay to them that, according to CNNMoney.com, in the month of January 2008, seventeen thousand jobs were lost here in America or when I tell them that the number of people applying for unemployment benefits increased by seventy-one thousand, the most since 2005, they respond by telling me, "Mike, it is all just a part of life; you have to work somewhere, and plus I like my job. I can't do anything differently anyway. I pay a lot of bills and I have to make sure they're paid each month. It hurts to hear "I can't." I can't do better, I can't become a business owner, I can't become a singer because my mom leaves me at home to take care of all my brothers and sister, and I can't own my own website and sell items on that website because my mind is on going to clubs, partying, and other unproductive activity.

I'm still speaking to every child who is reading this book (I hope you are still reading), I'm speaking to every mother, every father, every person of all ethnic groups, all faiths, everyone that knows that there is a better way—everyone that has keys but just can't find them. I'm speaking to you today, everyone that lost hope, today I tell you that's OK. I'm speaking to you, all of those who have an ear, I'm speaking to you, everyone that's stuck with major and minor problems, bad relationships, drug addictions, no money or not enough money, all that are in the category of hurt, pain, and on the brink of giving up, this is for you.

Those keys that David had established something great for Solomon, and that something established hope for all that read his story. It was great that David passed the keys of entrepreneurship to Solomon, and it was even greater that Solomon expressed his entrepreneurship through David's legacy, but it is a historic event that both decided that moment, over all opposition and all resistance, to change their diagram in the afflatus moment over their no. The years that I am calling "the Meshach and Camden Years" are similar to those of Solomon where he experienced destiny on the high end of the spectrum From David's legacy.

The afflatus moment of one's life is when he becomes inspired to do what seems to be abnormal to someone else after he has first accepted the opportunity to do so. Some may feel that it is totally impossible for that to happen in a moment. Well, what about those seventeen thousand people that lost their job in January of 2008? I would almost guarantee that some of those people working on that job worked on it for several years before being fired.

What about these major companies that decide that their multimillion-dollar industry would do better if they move overseas to make more millions, while you stand in another unemployment line as time goes by? To some of us that don't believe that, the moment I will become inspired is the moment I will become different in how I see myself, as the person that finds the nine-to-five normal and anything else abnormal. I don't know exactly when Solomon decided he would be a little abnormal, but the quality of his success moved right along as destiny required.

What do you require of yourself today? For Solomon it was wisdom, wealth and his writings (entrepreneurship). David carried those very important keys that sparked all of this just from a moment, the "afflatus moment." The jobs that were lost in early January 2008 tell me the importance of moving about on your own, discovering your passion, and finding entrepreneurship to be that of a joyous moment in life. It was so difficult and downright hard to break through those unbreakable times in my life when I didn't see the light at the end of the tunnel, not because it's not there, but because I was blind.

The whole take of me wanting, desiring, longing to be out and away from the nine-to-five system was similar to me thinking that the world is free from crime, and I could sleep at night with my screen door and my front door unlocked. It all seemed ridiculous to me. I skirmished back and forth with this thought that had me ridged with Yemi's so-inspired words of aspiration for my life. Yes, I was definitely inspired, but what's inspiration when your whole world is filled with personal problems that the whole world knows about?" I questioned myself precisely, standing still in that hot, unbearable place called a parking deck. Yemi wasn't like me. She is a woman from Africa, full of every positive point, with nothing to lose but distractions that show up like an unexpected bill that you toss on your coffee table, or better yet the floor of your living room. Just like the gurus, those CEOs, and those business owners of those multimillion-dollar industries, I just couldn't get away from the idea of money.

The idea of money was more important to me than questioning if there is really a better way. I did not compare my question to her words of inspiration, nor did I stand in limbo, aimlessly thinking my life would completely stop. I moved on. My forward progress was my thought of living. "I just wanted to live better," I thought continuously to myself.

The more I moved forward, the more I was presented mentally with this "moment entity," this opportunity to change the diagram of my life in an instant. I didn't want to be disturbed, I didn't feel like being bothered, but yet I was experiencing both while standing like a statue, feeling nothing but the scorch of the heat that reminded me, everyday, that as long as I'm in the system I would not experience any relief from the scorch of this relentless heat.

It would eventually play itself out over a course of time, but, not knowing Max Frisch great quote which states, "Time does not change us it just unfold us," I sat in emptiness, believing without a doubt that a certain amount of time would straighten out all of my unstable mindsets.

The more I lived, the more I was being stretched out—it seemed like to the limit—while desiring a better way, something new, no more getting up early, no dragging into work during those evening hours hearing "Arnold" instead of "Michael," having to hear we weren't the security guards they expected us to be but yet we did our job according to the handbook, forbidding us to talk unless we were on break—all of this was disheartening to me, a disgrace, as a worker in the system.

"How in the hell was my life supposed to be different?" The questions bore down on me, pushing, straining everything that inquired me to get past my slumping state. My sight was forward, but my vision wasn't; it had left sometime ago when my thought perished right along with my confidence to believe. This was the day after I decided that Yemi's words had been very inspiring, but not enough to banish my lifestyle of wrong-doing. I focused on changing my diagram then, seeing Yemi's words as they really were—life-changing.

I couldn't bear the thought of another thought coming, so I wanted to jolt my brain somehow and focus on something else. The sun walked backwards until it blanketed itself behind the light blue clouds that finally diminished as night was called into the seven o'clock hour. I sat contentedly in the driver's seat of my car, thinking mainly about Yemi and her constant battle to overcome, when suddenly I jumped, almost banging the side of my body on my car door trying to get out of there when I saw the door open into the parking deck where I was located. "What's up, Yemi? You scared me, girl!"

"I knew I would get you, Arnold," she said laughing, walking to my place of embarrassment.

"So how is everything today, Yemi?" I asked. Like I had become accustomed to, in an instant a smile adorned my face as I prepared for words of life from her mouth to proceed and touch me as they usually did.

"I'm fine, Arnold. So how is your mother?"

"She's OK, thanks for asking."

"Did you enroll in school like you promised you would do, Arnold?"

"To be honest, I didn't, but before you say it, I am going to. You don't have to worry about that." I said that carefully, knowing that if I said the wrong thing she would really lay it on me.

"Arnold, your life is too important to keep putting it off. You have to do it now; God helps those who help themselves." I knew it was coming: her correction, her desire to see me do something besides working security, coming in day after day with the opportunity to change my diagram but lying to myself.

"Arnold, I know you get tired of me saying this, but you have to be serious about you life. I came from Africa and I could not speak English, but I said I would keep trying. Arnold, I won't be here forever, and I don't want to leave and come back to this building and see you still working here!"

"I'm not going to be working here Yemi, God is going to help me get out of here." She looked at me as if I told her the sky was red, she stared at me, then she put both of her lips together, pressed hard, and released, coming to a complete relaxation. "Arnold, if you're not going to go to school, you need to figure out what you can do."

"I want to go to school, Yemi, I just got to make some time. That's all."

"Arnold, look at us."

My smile turned into a contortion with no chance of that smile returning. I became all ears. "I'm serious, Arnold, they don't care about us, they just want to work the hell out of us and we get nothing! We are better than this, Arnold, and God says we are better than this! They treat us so badly here, Arnold, and we don't deserve this. One day soon I am going to be a chemist. That's why I am going to school. God has given me the opportunity when no one else did, Arnold, and I am taking it!" I swallowed just to keep from shedding a tear.

"I will see you next break, Arnold."

"Ok, Yemi." I stood there feeling like something was changing, but I didn't know what. As I watched her go from that parking deck back to the main lobby of the building where we worked, in an instant I felt like

I wanted to do something, anything, just to not be a part of the system any more. The more I dwelled on this moment of inspiration, the more I felt as though the world of old was become that perfect world. The world before the fall of man, that world that says that everyone is equal to do anything that they want to do, the world that upholds, giving life again, replacing those dandelions that died from the heat of the summer with brand-new ones that grow from the summer heat. I said to myself over and over again, "I'm better than this; thank you God for this job, but I'm better than this. There is more for me than just this, coming here and not getting anything out of it but a paycheck."

As time passed, those words were like runners in a marathon—I couldn't get them out of my head. I could hear Yemi's words start to change my diagram. This was the first time during my years conformed to the nine-to-five system that I became inspired to do something about this. This, in fact, was my afflatus moment.

People were coming and going, gaining and losing their jobs. Many people did not want to disconnect from the system, so therefore their outbursts told who they were and how much they wanted to get out.

Additional months passed, and the poems that I wrote to myself became my all and all. Whenever I could get a chance, at work or at home, I wrote poems as if I was writing out of my mind. I felt so overwhelmed in working these poems into a section of my life that was creditable to a positive attribute. I couldn't see it then, but looking back on it today, Yemi was the embodiedment of something that was before our time. She didn't just occupy my empty space with hope and passion to run on through my afflatus moment, but she drew others around her to see the light that encompassed her atmosphere and in return influenced all that saw this light.

More time passed, and more poems grew, until the day I found them to be boring and somewhat of a "had to do" thing for me. I wasn't attempting to give up on them yet, but I was awfully close to it.

That parking deck that I found myself guarding more than anything else in my life at that time was beginning to make me feel as though I was going insane, so just to make sure I wasn't really insane, I walked out of that dull boring security booth and found the inside of my seat to be a sanity haven for me when I felt as if I was going over the edge. (All of us do feel like that at times) I thought long and hard, and my focus slowly shifted into a different direction, a direction that was taking me on a course that I had no idea that would exist in my life. I sat in that car assessing ideas of all that occurred on and off my job, wondering when all of the wonderful thoughts would start manifesting clearly. I smiled when I came across one of my poems lying on the floor on the passenger's side of my car; although I was experiencing the afflatus moment, I wasn't half inspired to write poetry anymore after about a month into it.

"God, what can I do? What do I have left? This is the best thing that I have come in contact with thus far, but I lost my edge for it." I picked up a blank piece of paper laying on my seat after those words knocked on heaven door, waiting on God to listen to them. I thought if he took time to listen to my statement, then I wouldn't feel so confused, and why I was so caught up in this moment but consumed by abandonment of my new recreation poetry that was killing the moment.

"Come on God, what is it? Why do I feel so discouraged? I know something has to work out for me, so what is it!" The same frustration that I heard in Yemi's voice when school became more of a burden than a blessing, when the job we worked on didn't serve a purpose, but an unresponsiveness that was a device to kill that very purpose—I heard it. That's not all I saw in the vision that evening. While weighing my thoughts of concern, I saw a will to overcome when overcoming wasn't a thing that she saw. I heard a cry for success among failure for years while in that prison. I heard her voice echo beyond barriers of defeat, yelling, "Overcoming is the way out and success is around the corner!"

I heard in my sleep that it's just a season of hurt and disappointment, but where there is one kind of season there is another kind of season. I smiled to myself, secretly, then tried to hide those tears that ran down my face unannounced, but I welcomed them anyway after my unsystematic thinking. It wasn't magic, an unexplained fairy tale that we tell to our children to make them smile so they will go to sleep comfortably at night, nor was it a fabricated story that we adults speak about in that spotlight moment—no, it wasn't that moment, but it was the afflatus moment. In an instant I knew what I wanted to do and what I was going to do; I was suddenly enlighten with just a blue ink pen and a white piece of notebook paper. I continued to allow myself to be overcome with the moment entity and how the afflatus moment (I didn't know it then, but God did) was changing the diagram of my life as I sat in my car and wrote a piece of what is now my first unpublished manuscript. I couldn't believe it: in just an instant I had turned my unresolved issue to a destiny.

I was so happy I couldn't contain it; somebody had to know about this moment, this "afflatus moment."

I knew Yemi wasn't working that day, so while waiting until the next day that she would be working, I spoke with several of my coworkers, showing them every bit of my inspired work that had me off of my rocker. While I continued to wear this uninterrupted smile, others made many attempts to interrupt that smile with statements like, "That sounds OK, but you need to work on your grammar." Others would say, "I hope you've got an editor, because I see a lot of mistakes." Or, "That's good that you are writing Mike, but make sure you go to school and take some classes before you get that book published."

I heard it all: the words coming from those I felt would encourage me discouraged me, while all along these people never talked about a better way, the Solomon Years, three demonstrations of destiny, or the six keys to entrepreneurship. They never spoke of any of these weapons that would place a hold on the system and free them up forever, not for my life but for their life. I ran with my moment and understood clearly that I wasn't giving up nor was I quitting; there is someone just like me that holds a strong grip on her destiny, and that's who I will talk to as long as I am here on this job.

"Arnold that is great, I am so proud of you. It sounds good, but let me tell you Arnold, you need a computer for the book."

"A computer? I don't know how to type, Yemi," I explained after my rapid heartbeat moved to a regular and more unhurried beat.

"Yes, a computer. You are a writer, and that's what writers use. OK, Arnold? The writing's good, you will make it, and I will be there to see you one day—not here, but that place of destiny."

I couldn't help but feel the emotions of a destined woman that was waiting on her manifestation to be brought to the forefront of her life, like a prophecy made visible over a period of time. My writing increased as more ideas came forth, building upon the manuscript from day to day. I thanked God daily for the gift and never neglected it when the path to its completion got hard and excruciating; instead I remained focused and let time unfold it. When the day came that I finally was able to get a computer (and I tell you the truth, it was a life saver), it worked out well without any problems to report.

"Arnold, that's wonderful. This is really a nice computer. Now just type until you learn how to type well."

"I didn't have the money to pay for it with cash, so I went the rent-a-center route."

"That's OK, it will work out."

A year went by, and the interacting that went on between us suddenly stopped. Yemi wasn't there anymore; her destiny led her out of the country. To this day I remember and I will never forget that she was the moment entity that sparked my afflatus moment. To all who are still reading, I say that the biggest weapon that you have against anything in life, especially the system, is the moment you become inspired to do something else that in return is a better way. This must have been the way Thomas Edison felt when the words that came out of his mouth didn't express defeat but triumph, when he boldly said, "I have not failed, I just found ten thousand ways that won't work." What a way to allow the afflatus moment, to keep on moving despite of the so-called failures that people say you are in.

Even now, as I sit here alone coming to the conclusion of this manuscript, there are many people who don't have my best interest at heart (a lot of you know what I'm talking about). They say that it won't work, what I'm doing is only for a certain group of people, my past is not that good, why don't I give up. I hear it all, but there is a voice that I hear that has been crying for the last four years, and it says don't give up, don't throw in the towel, your moment is here, in an instant your diagram is changing. That voice that cries out in me is also crying out in you as well, and that voice is called the "afflatus moment." Don't ignore it, walk in it!

Part 3

CHAPTER 17

In The End We Always Win!

Before we go into the last chapter of this book I want to say thank you to all of you that stuck around here for the last week, two weeks, three weeks, and for some of you days reading this book, it means the world to me. More than just that, I must say with all sincerity to those of you that have read this piece of work that it has been time consuming to me but helpful to you, I say thank you as well, and I'm so glad that God has given me something to write that would be so life-changing for you and me. I believe somewhere on our road to entrepreneurship—well, to be honest, not just entrepreneurship, but whatever destination you have in mind for your life—it is expectedly good to have someone in your life, or someone you're just meeting that can and will interject a life-changing moment in each and every one of our lives. For me, of course you already know, it was the young lady who worked with me named Yemi. Living the vision that you have envisioned, not anyone else, but you have set in place with the help of God, he has set you on a course that will bring enormous joy that no man can take away.

That's important—not so much the joy, since we do have some parts of our life that are not of a joyous situation, but I'm speaking mainly about the vision that sets us on course, where we need to be.

I had major trouble with that growing up, and some even after my afflatus moment, but fortunately my moment didn't end when Yemi and I never communicated again. Sharing our destinies with each other was just beginning. Seventeen thousand employees lost their jobs in the month of January of 2008. That doesn't make a bit of difference to some people, seeing that they have their jobs, and the flow of their commitment to that job is commendable in the sight of those who are in management, but where there are employees, there lies one paycheck from being... let's just say, where you don't want to be. Just like those seventeen thousand employees that lost their jobs, so can we, those of us that are a part of that system. But as time had elapsed on those employees in just a moment, there is another moment, a moment that doesn't hinge on your past but on the moment you decide to change—the first moment.

I grew up in an era where church was a definite must, which was something that my mom didn't play around with. What I mean by that is, she was serious about us going; so serious that all day Sunday, Wednesday night, and revival seasons (five or six times a year) were all reserved for church.

You're talking about a pain in the you-know-what! I can't elaborate on it enough. All that church seemed to be more than I could handle, but not in my mother's view. She was consistent, holding on to her observation that said to my sister and I, "As long as you are in this house and as long as those doors are open, you will go to church. It's going to help you in the long run of your life." (How aching and painful as a child; but I lived.) I managed to push through what was, I thought, to be a very boring event growing up. Nothing there appeased me in the slightest—except maybe when I heard the pastor say, "Alright everyone, stand for the benediction, we're ready to go home!"

Those were the words that I heard that sat me in isolation during my church days growing up as a youth, largely because there wasn't substance that I could hear, take in, live by, and grow from—maybe because I didn't have a hearing ear. Today is much different. I have a clear ear to hear what could have an impact on not where I am today but where I'm going.

Where I was going in 2004 was great and Yemi was a great asset to that but without someone like Yemi your confidence in pursuing your destiny could get a little dim. During the time that destiny was pulling Yemi closer to herself, I found myself more than ever to at least have a couple church services a month—seeing that I wasn't that enthused by the entire cooperation, since most of them I have attended in my life have been solely focused on business revenue instead of physical empowerment—with that said, my ears was closed but my eyes were open.

I had an opportunity to grow up with a mother who is blind, but her ability to hear was far greater than my ability to see. If it wasn't, I would not have tried so many underhanded things as a child, thinking that I would outsmart her blindness.

"I didn't go in the refrigerator, Ma!"

"You did because I *heard* you! Get yourself in that room, and that's where you will stay the rest of the day for lying!"

That was my mom's word of discipline and my poor job of lying through my words of dishonesty. (Those two didn't match up very well, and I found myself not bouncing back very well.) I heard something different something that was transparent; words that confirmed where I was going.

Seeing something and hearing something kind of work hand-in-hand like a motor and a transmission, or team members on a team trying to make a big shot, but just like different levels of players on that team, different acts of those ball players are viewed for their various playing skills. That's how I recall the two senses sight and hearing. For instance, sight would be like a movie you watch and obtain all the information based on what you saw, but hearing is a little different. Hearing is like a book you read, and all the information is based on what you read. In my opinion, hearing would be like having the best basketball player on a team; that player is versatile, he makes the right decision based on what he has learned, not on what he has seen, and that basketball player reads (hears) about a play that the other team has drawn up against him and acts accordingly, not what he has seen but what he has read (hear).

To my wonderful children out there that want to advance in school and receive the best education that you can receive, lend your ear to all the books that you possibly can read. To all of my soon-to-be entrepreneurs, hearing is important; no one will never know that more then you. Just seeing your vision is good, but hearing over and over again that it will work is even better, saying to yourself that all six keys of entrepreneurship have already been placed inside of you by God, and you will succeed because of it is hearing in action and it will work on your behalf.

The middle part of 2005, hearing a word really exploited and confirmed my "afflatus moment." I was encouraged by a young lady to do something that was out of my normal element.

"Mike, I know that you like your church and all of that but if you would just give my church a try I promise you everything will change."

"What do you mean by that?" She and I had several conversations in the past about some personal problems I was having with my church at that time, so I had an idea where she would be going with this.

"I believe we have the best church in the world, and if you visit one Sunday, you will never want leave." She said.

"Never leave —what church is that?"

"The name of my church is New Birth Charlotte. It's the best, Mike."

"That's what they all say just to get members; they all claim to be good!"

"I'm serious, Mike. Just come out one Sunday and hear our pastor's messages."

"How can you say that if I come to your church I won't ever leave? My church is just as good as yours!"

The more we talked that evening, the more I got fervent about her statements concerning her so-impressive church.

"Mike, I'm not going to argue with you, all I'm trying to say is that when you hear these messages, your life with change so much that you will not want to leave. That's all."

"All those big churches want is money, and you know that. Why don't you leave and come to my church?" I added.

We went on for another five or ten minutes until she had all she could take. "Mike, this has gone on too long, and I can't talk to you without you trying to debate. I think it would be best if we stop talking, period."

"Whatever you say. I knew you weren't my friend anyway." I yelled.

The dial tone was a permanent ringing in my ear. She was totally sincere about her future of no conversation with me. It ended before it got started. My life went on from a part of me that hurt mentally. Everyone that was in my life wasn't positive. Just like me, they were barely making it, and my desire to write was slowly being taking from me right under my nose by people that said I couldn't do it. After my "afflatus moment" because of my constant involvement in things that weren't right, I felt hopeless, and my writing would weaken under a hand that cared more about damaging activity than optimistic destiny.

The more I tried, the more I found myself falling back to what I was into such as the club life, internet dating, false hope, no money, and not ever experiencing anything different since everything was the same. Finally, after a terrible Saturday night, I got up Sunday morning and decided I would see if there was a website for this church she called New Birth Charlotte. By no means did I want to relive that Saturday night, so one way or the other I would try to put it behind me with maybe going to a different church, since I left the one that I invited the New Birth member to go to.

Before the website was up completely (mainly because my computer was slow), I heard words put together eloquently that geared toward empowerment. I felt everything inside me and around me start to change. An hour later, to my surprise, the pastor of the church wasn't there, but the message that was preached spoke to the bad time that I had the previous night and how I would be able to overcome it. It was amazing.

Time moved on, and the messages that were preached by the pastor of New Birth were of hope, love, and most of all empowerment. I would learn later his name is Pastor Terrell Murphy of this New Birth Charlotte church. I never in a million years would have thought, when she told me that I would be there forever if I ever visited, that I would say that she was right. Well, she was right.

CHAPTER 18

Conclusion

It's important that we that stress so hard within ourselves that, to occupy that new way and see a complete turn around in our life, we must be quick to hear as well as doers of the vision. I never had to see Pastor Murphy or Yemi to desire to excel from the words of empowerment that they spoke in my life that would get me pass the cubicle and into the lap of the executive chair—I just had to be available to hear each of them.

So many times we want to be a part of something as long as we can catch sight of it, but when you decide to lay down a legacy for those that are coming after you, you have to spend a lot of time listening—first listening to yourself, then those that believe in your dream.

During some of Pastor Murphy's messages (because I was focused on hearing and not seeing) I was able to soak up so much information and use it for my life, and no one ever knew it simply because I was hearing what he was saying. Something he said in a recent message was, and I'm quoting him, "It's not that you are stuck, it's just that your destiny is just that great." What I got from that is that we, as people of destiny, have to go through the fires of life to get to the eternal destiny, and sometimes going through that fire we seem to be stuck, but we are not.

Entrepreneurship is not easy, and we make it even harder by giving up on it. There has been a recent drop-off in our economy, so much so that people are losing their homes and going into foreclosure, gas is at its highest ever this year than any year since the war, jobs are picking up and going overseas, businesses are getting bought out for nothing hardly but a bottle of water and a hot dog, and what we are calling it is a recession. Things that we depended on to survive or just wanted but couldn't afford, like that fifty-thousand-dollar car or that two-hundred-thousand-dollar home, after you get finished paying for them, you would have paid double and in some cases triple!

All that we have is going up in smoke in this recession, this collapse of the economy, the down-turning of money from a plus to a minus in all working class citizens. This recession has just begun with the collapse of the financial system and the rise of gas prices, but it started in the mind of those that settled for the nine-to-five and never attempted to push an effort in the direction of entrepreneurship.

One quote from a movie that I heard recently states, "He doesn't own his own company so they own him." Whatever you don't own can affect you in a negative way, and that's what has happened with this recession. If we want to overcome the nine-to-five syndrome, we first have to hear over and over again in our minds, "Entrepreneurship." Even as you read this to yourselves, believe it on a daily basis and don't waver with those critics who will try to persuade you that what you are doing isn't going to work. A couple of days ago someone told me that the competition that I have against me in writing a book like this is very great, and he advised me to put it on a shelf and start writing something that people want to hear or else I won't make any money.

I laughed, then made it perfectly clear to him that this book is not about how much money I can make, but how many entrepreneurs this book will make out of people. My pastor said something that was so timely to us (the church), and I use it today in some of the things that I do. That is, "Start somewhere. Wherever you are in life, start right there." If you are at a job and you know one day you want to be an entrepreneur, don't let that job discourage you. Start right there, if you feel as though college will have an impact on you moving into entrepreneurship; start right there. Don't be afraid to start somewhere. That job, that nine-to-five, may disappear one day, but your desire to reach the highest place in your life won't, so just keep pushing toward that mark so that you will be able to help someone else in the future. Forty-seven million people in the USA don't have healthcare. The reason is simple: we can't afford it. It's an answer to that problem. If you and I can take hold of the keys of entrepreneurship, then that list of forty-seven million without healthcare will go down.

The hope lies with you and me, how much of this book will we adhere to, and how much of it we ignore thinking this is just another inspiring book. But those twenty-five thousand people that broke away from the system to create their own way heard something, and what they heard was, "There is a better way." To everyone, including my children, there is a way that we all can have a better life and overcome the nine-to-five system, feeding off of our afflatus moments, hearing positive things from people who care about you and where you're going, and finally saying to ourselves: In The End We Always Win!

The End

Jenni Wheeler designed the cover and the interior layout for this book. You did a great job. Thanks for allowing more time for me to iron out all the kinks Jenni. Special thanks to Belinda Jackson who did the revised editing on this book. Without your hand of expertise, I would have been lost. You did a tremendous job.

In a time of need God surely does provide, thank you God for placing all the key components in place to make this all come to pass.

Printed in the United States
137969LV00005B/6/P